WRITING
WORKSHOP

PROMOTING
COLLEGE SUCCESS

Linda Lonon Blanton
Linda Lee

Heinle & Heinle Publishers

I(T)P   An International Thomson Publishing Company

Albany • Bonn • Boston • Cincinnati • Detroit • London • Madrid • Melbourne
Mexico City • New York • Pacific Grove • Paris • San Francisco • Tokyo • Toronto • Washington

The publication of *Writing Workshop: Promoting College Success* was directed by the members of the Newbury House Publishing Team at Heinle & Heinle:

Erik Gundersen, Editorial Director
Jonathan Boggs, Market Development Director
Mike Burggren, Production Services Coordinator

Also participating in the publication of this program were:

Publisher: Stanley J. Galek
Assistant Editor: Jill Kinkade
Associate Market Development Director: Mary Sutton
Manufacturing Coordinator: Mary Beth Hennebury
Project Manager: Angela Malovich Castro, English Language Trainers
Cover Artist: Mike Burggren
Cover Designer: Bortman Design Group

Heinle & Heinle Publishers is a division of International Thomson Publishing, Inc.

Manufactured in the United States of America.

ISBN 0-8384-7973-1

10   9   8   7   6   5   4   3   2   1

A Special Thanks

The authors and publisher would like to thank the following individuals who reviewed and/or field-tested *The Multicultural Workshop* and/or *Writing Workshop: Promoting College Success* at various stages during the development of the series and who offered many helpful insights and suggestions:

Peggy Anderson, *Wichita State University*
Vivian Wind Aronow, *College of Staten Island (City University of New York)*
Luke Bailey, *University of Hawaii at Hilo*
Kathleen Beauchene, *Community College of Rhode Island*
Cheryl Benz, *Miami-Dade Community College*
Bernadette Garcia Budd, *Suffolk County Community College (NJ)*
Elizabeth Byleen, *University of Kansas*
Tom Coles, *Arizona State University*
Danielle Dibie, *California State University, Northridge*
Kathleen Flynn, *Glendale College (CA)*
Virginia Gibbons, *Oakton Community College (IL)*
Virginia Heringer, *Pasadena City College*
Helen Harper, *American Language Institute, New York University*
Pat Holdcraft, *University of Miami*
Wendy Hyman-Fite, *Washington University in St. Louis*
Joyce Kling, *Harvard University*
Sally LaLuzerne-Oi, *Hawaii Pacific University*
Lorin Leith, *Santa Rosa Junior College (CA)*
Martha Grace Low, *University of Oregon*
Sheila McKee, *University of North Texas*
Joe McVeigh, *University of Southern California*
Judith L. Paiva, *Northern Virginia Community College*
Meredith Pike-Baky, *University of California, Berkeley & San Francisco Unified School District*
Heather Robertson, *Glendale College (CA)*
Julietta Ruppert, *Houston Community College*
Adrianne Saltz, *Boston University*
Eve Chambers Sanchez, *Oregon State University*
Charles Schroen, *The Pennsylvania State University*
Marilyn Spaventa, *Santa Barbara City College*
Betty Speyrer, *Delgado Community College (LA)*
Lois Spitzer, *Atlantic Community College (NJ)*
Brad Stocker, *Miami-Dade Community College*
Fredericka Stoller, *Northern Arizona University*
Elizabeth Templin, *University of Arizona*
Marjorie Vai, *The New School for Social Research (NY)*
Virginia Vogel Zanger, *Boston Public Schools*

CONTENTS

Many college writing assignments require students to interpret something they have read or seen. In this workshop, you will look at one person's interpretation of a movie and then write your own interpretation of a short story.

Reading Selections: *The Garden of the Finzi-Continis* (a movie review)
Night (a short story by Bret Lott)

Strategies: Interpreting • Analyzing • Previewing • Writing Margin Notes • Using Context • Quickwriting • Organizing Ideas • Evaluating • Revising

Grammar Workshop 1: a) adjective clauses b) appositives

Workshop Two: Summarizing Nonfiction

Summarizing is involved in many kinds of college writing assignments. In this workshop, you will read a magazine article and then evaluate several summaries of the article. Finally, you will choose an article of interest to you and write a brief summary of it.

Reading Selection: *Friends, Good Friends—And Such Good Friends* (an essay by Judith Viorst)

Strategies: Previewing • Writing Margin Notes • Using Context • Making Your Thesis Clear • Analyzing • Summarizing • Evaluating • Revising

Grammar Workshop 2: a) noun clauses with "that"
b) reported speech

Workshop Three: Writing in Response to Reading

In your college coursework, you may be asked to read an article and answer a question about it in writing. In this workshop, you will have the chance to read sample responses to questions and then write your own response to a text-based question.

Reading Selection: *Sample essay responses*

Strategies: Paraphrasing • Analyzing • Comparing • Writing Margin Notes • Evaluating • Quickwriting • Making Your Thesis Clear • Organizing Ideas • Evaluating • Revising

Grammar Workshop 3: a) *it's* + adjective + infinitive   b) gerunds as subjects

Workshop Four: Incorporating Others' Ideas Into Your Writing

In college courses, you will be expected to incorporate others' ideas and research into your writing. How do you do this? In this workshop, you will learn to cite or document sources, report on research, and evaluate new ideas, all within the framework of your own thinking.

Reading Selection: *Seven Keys to Learning* (a magazine article)

Strategies: Previewing • Writing Margin Notes • Using Context • Analyzing • Using Quotations • Citing Sources • Paraphrasing • Synthesizing • Revising

Grammar Workshop 4: a) adverb clauses   b) reduced adverb clauses

Workshop Five: Using Writing to Understand a Text

In many college courses, you will be required to read extensively. In this workshop, you will experiment with ways to use writing to understand a text. You will also try different strategies that can help you to manage long reading assignments.

Reading Selection: *Stimulating Beverages* (a science textbook excerpt)

Strategies: Previewing • Analyzing • Identifying the Writer's Thesis • Using Context • Writing Margin Notes • Underlining • Quickwriting • Revising

Grammar Workshop 5: a) word forms b) rearranging information c) sentence beginnings

Workshop Six: Responding to Exam Questions

On examinations in your academic courses, you will have to show your knowledge of course material. In most cases, your instructor will evaluate your responses based on how clearly, accurately, and comprehensively you answer the questions. In this workshop, you will look at different kinds of exam questions, evaluate several exam responses, and then practice writing your own answers to typical exam questions.

Reading Selection: *Sample exam responses*

Strategies: Analyzing • Evaluating • Synthesizing • Organizing Ideas

Grammar Workshop 6: a) parallel forms b) conjunctive adverbs

Workshop Seven: Reporting on Research

Much academic writing consists of reporting on research. In this workshop, you will become more familiar with the format and organization of different types of research reports. You will then carry out a very short research assignment and report on it in writing.

Reading Selection: *Working With Gilly* (an academic report)

Strategies: Applying What You Know • Classifying • Previewing • Writing Margin Notes • Taking Notes • Analyzing • Revising

Grammar Workshop 7: sentence variety

At different times during your academic career, you may have to take a test of your writing ability. The purpose of these tests is to find out how well you can communicate your ideas in writing. In this workshop, you will explore some of the criteria that instructors use to evaluate students' essays on a writing test. You will also look at some sample writing test responses and have the chance to take several practice tests.

Reading Selection: *Sample writing test responses*

Strategies: Analyzing • Evaluating • Making Your Thesis Clear

GUIDE TO STRATEGIES

Overview

Writing Workshop: Promoting College Success is a textbook for students who are preparing to enter the academic mainstream and who will soon need to function without preparatory-program or developmental-writing assistance. English may be their first or second language.

Writing Workshop is the fourth in a series of textbooks designed to comprehensively meet the needs of college and college-bound readers and writers. The complete program includes the following titles:

- *The Multicultural Workshop, Book 1*   high beginning

- *The Multicultural Workshop, Book 2*   intermediate

- *The Multicultural Workshop, Book 3*   high intermediate

- *Writing Workshop: Promoting College Success*   advanced

These four textbooks are augmented by *The Multicultural Workshop Box,* a self-paced reading program with 100 additional, authentic readings on laminated cards. *The Box* contains works of fiction by writers like Maya Angelou and Gary Soto, as well as journalistic selections from publications like *The New York Times* and *Parade Magazine.*

Focus and Framework

Writing Workshop assumes that collaboration and communication are powerful tools for learning; hence, a format of interactive workshops. The pedagogy of *Writing Workshop* also assumes that social contexts shape how and why writers write, and that, in school, writing takes place to accomplish academic tasks. So, using these materials, students write and read in ways and for purposes expected in college courses.

Of note: some teachers may think that students with basic grammar and writing problems are not yet ready to confront academic writing. Experience tells us, however, that all aspects of writing, both large and small, are learned best when students are using writing for authentic purposes. In *Writing Workshop,* these authentic purposes take the form of actual college-writing activities.

Writing Workshop follows *The Multicultural Workshop, Books 1–3,* but it can easily stand alone. *Writing Workshop* applies the same basic pedagogy, but it is more advanced, more focused on writing, and is designed for all developing writers, whether first- or second-language speakers of English.

While *The Multicultural Workshop, Books 1–3,* develop much of the critical literacy students need for academic success, *Writing Workshop* completes the job by applying critical literacy to *real* and *specific* college-writing assignments. It draws from mainstream coursework, allowing students to get their feet wet—even jump in—but with the assistance of their teacher and peers.

Goals of *Writing Workshop*

In preparing students for mainstream coursework, the specific goals of *Writing Workshop* are to:

- prepare students to get over the assessment hurdles that stand between them and a mainstream curriculum

- promote critical reading, writing, and thinking

- enable the use of strategies necessary to meet future academic demands

- familiarize students with the kinds of academic assignments found in coursework across the disciplines

- assist students in trying authentic academic assignments on for size

- lessen anxiety about future coursework by showing developing writers how successful college students read and write to meet mainstream course assignments, and how they can do so too.

Contents of *Writing Workshop*

Readings in *Writing Workshop* come from a variety of academic disciplines (economics, linguistics, film studies, geography, literature, education, botany, psychology, and biology). The writing tasks, however, are based on the kinds of assignments that form the basis for all college coursework, regardless of discipline.

In *Writing Workshop,* students gain experience in, among other things:

- writing long-answer (essay) exams

- writing timed responses on proficiency-type exams

- researching topics students themselves formulate

- responding to textbook readings

- writing summaries and short-answer exams

- activating prior knowledge to make sense of new ideas and information

- analyzing and writing academic reports

- planning and writing multi-draft essays

Why these activities? Because mainstream college students across the disciplines engage in them, and, because to enter the mainstream and succeed, developing writers must learn to engage in them too.

Strategies Developed in *Writing Workshop*

The development of writing, reading, and critical thinking strategies is given special emphasis in *Writing Workshop*. We believe it is important for student writers to develop a repertoire of strategies, as well as the language for talking about them. Selected strategies are highlighted in each workshop and cross-referenced to explanations and examples in the Reference Guide at the back of the book. A complete list of these strategies is provided on page ix.

Acknowledgments

We are grateful to the following faculty at the University of New Orleans, who provided expert advise to us on writing-reading demands in their respective disciplines: Dr. Ron Greene, Research Professor in Physics; Dr. Martha Ward, Research Professor in Anthropology; Myles Hassell, Instructor in Business and English; the late Dr. Kristian Preston, Associate Professor in Geography; Dr. Laura Serpa, Associate Professor in Geology and Geophysics; Dr. Mackie Blanton, Associate Professor in Linguistics; and Dr. John Utley, Professor in Biological Sciences. For their many wonderful insights and ideas during the development of the project, we thank the reviewers listed at the beginning of this book.

We are also grateful to our editor Erik Gundersen, for his friendship and support, and to the many students who assisted us, especially Linda Treash, Jennifer Kuchta, Michelle Graci, and Kiril Milanov.

Based on the tenets of collaborative learning and literacy acquisition theory, a workshop approach is task-based and interactive. To complete tasks, students read, write, and talk. In this context, language use becomes purposeful, a means to an end. Meaningful communication, in turn, requires interaction. Hence, the workshop classroom, with its shared tasks, peer work, discussions, and reader-response groups. Below are tips for using *Writing Workshop* in the classroom.

❖ ORIENTING STUDENTS TO A WORKSHOP APPROACH

To many students, a workshop approach may be new. As a result of prior instruction, they may enter the class with the point of view that every scrap of writing must not only be read but corrected by the teacher; the teacher has all the answers; and their peers have nothing to teach them. None of this is true in a workshop classroom.

We urge you to explain to students that a workshop methodology is theoretically sound; that it has been successfully field-tested with students like them; that active participation is central to successful learning; and that any new approach takes some getting used to. Based on the adage "Try it. You'll like it," ask them to give workshops a chance.

To teachers unused to a workshop approach, we offer the same advice. While it may take a while to "get the hang" of it, we urge you not to abandon the approach even if things seem difficult the first or second time around. Explain the task, model ways of responding, and talk students through it. Let students know it's normal to have difficulty with something new, and then carry on.

❖ WORKING IN GROUPS

- Groups of three or four work best.

- With a diverse class, mix linguistic and cultural backgrounds.

- Mix strengths and weaknesses.

- To get the mixes indicated above, you may need to assign students to groups.

- Sometimes it works to keep the same groups together for several activities in a row, for the duration of a whole workshop, or even for an entire school term. It all depends on the learning styles and personalities of individuals and groups. In general, though, peer work is more effective when students begin to know each other's interests, personalities, and writing needs.

- Insist on a "good neighbor" policy: all contributions deserve respect; everyone gets a turn; everyone's input is welcomed, even required; everyone needs assistance and feedback; and making errors is "no big deal."

- Circulate during group work, consulting with groups that call for help. When you see praiseworthy group work, acknowledge it: the dynamics of positive group work get learned this way.

❖ USING THE REFERENCE GUIDE

Becoming aware of writing, reading, and critical thinking strategies and learning how to use them are important goals of *Writing Workshop*. Key strategies that students use in each workshop lesson are cross-referenced to explanations and examples in a Reference Guide at the back of the book.

Encourage your students to use the Reference Guide. It answers What? How? Why? and When? questions about the strategies and provides helpful information about using them. Students on the verge of mainstream coursework need to build an arsenal of useful strategies; time spent with the Reference Guide furthers this process. In addition, the guide serves as a mini-handbook, leaving the body of the textbook uncluttered and free of the instructional apparatus that often gets in students' way.

❖ **DEALING WITH COLLEGE-LEVEL TEXTS**

At first glance, workshop readings may appear too difficult for students to handle. Keep in mind, though, that students are neither being asked to "learn" the readings, nor model their writing after them. Instead, students are asked to *interact* with the readings, by performing various tasks on them. Even texts "over readers' heads" can be accessed, if the right instructional scaffolding is provided, and the readers learn ways "in." This is the time—when help can be provided—for students to learn to deal with difficult texts.

❖ **USING** *THE MULTICULTURAL WORKSHOP BOX*

The Multicultural Workshop Box, a resource containing a hundred readings, is available as a companion to *Writing Workshop.* Designed to bring the library into the classroom, the box holds laminated reading cards, charts for recording students' progress, and answer keys to the questions on each card. Graded by level of difficulty, the readings in the box range from easy to challenging.

 The Multicultural Workshop Box provides a number of benefits to students using *Writing Workshop:* it provides additional readings; it motivates students by providing choices and a sense of self-direction; and it offers further activities to reinforce strategies used in the textbook.

 One way to use *The Multicultural Workshop Box* is to designate a class period as "free reading day," with students working independently with readings from the box. Or, if students have access to a separate reading laboratory, they can be encouraged, or required, to read from the box outside of class, on their own time. Either use of the box fosters independent learning, creates opportunities for additional reading experience, and can provide a basis for group discussions.

❖ **BUILDING WRITING FOLDERS**

For each of the eight workshops in the book, students complete a writing assignment, which they place in their writing folders. Some writings enter the folder in rougher stages than others; not every piece of writing needs to be worked through to a polished state in order to be of value to its writer.

 Here are writing folders "in a nutshell":

- Each student needs his or her own writing folder. A manila folder works fine.

- At the end of each workshop, a writing goes into the student's folder.

- All drafts should be dated and identified by workshop number. For multi-draft work, the writing should also be identified by draft number.

- Peer conferences and teacher-student conferences are essential during and after the drafting process.

- Students should be free to return to any piece of writing in their folder for further drafting or student-teacher conferencing, even when further drafting is not assigned.

- In providing feedback and evaluation, consider that a writer's clear focus, thorough development of ideas, lucid expression, and authentic voice are fully as important as grammatical accuracy.

- By the end of the academic term, students should be prepared to pick out two or three of their multi-draft writings and work them into as polished a state as possible.

❖ PROVIDING FEEDBACK

It is axiomatic that archers improve in accuracy only when they see how far from the target their shots have fallen. The same is true of student writers. Feedback is essential to them. The following are suggestions for improving this aspect of writing instruction.

To provide feedback, confer with each student individually during the drafting period. This may mean conferencing one-on-one after class or holding mini-conferences in class while students are writing. However you choose to do it, students will want and need individualized attention and direction.

Keep in mind that developing writers are in the process of *becoming*. The process is not instantaneous nor always open to instruction, and it involves constant adjustment on the writer's part. As experienced writing teachers well know, it also requires patience, goodwill, and endurance on the teacher's part.

Peer feedback is valuable too, and is suggested throughout *Writing Workshop,* but students need training in knowing how to give it. Fearful of hurting their peers' feelings, they often consider all writing "good." To respond insightfully, students need to know which questions to ask themselves as they analyze a piece of writing. These questions need to be the same ones their teacher asks in providing feedback and/or evaluating student writing (see suggestions below). We recommend modeling a feedback session to help students "get the hang of it."

❖ EVALUATING WRITING

We suggest the following questions as a basis for your own evaluation of students' writing (and for student responses to each other's writing):

- Does the writer say something significant? (Significance may lie in saying something new, or something "old" in a fresh, new way.)

- Is the writer developing a distinct voice?

- Does the writer reach beyond simply reporting events to interpreting and analyzing them?

- Is the writer's focus limited enough for the length of the paper?

- Does the writer show an awareness of audience?

- Is the writing clear?

- Does the writer make the topic interesting? Are details vivid? Are examples relevant?

- Can a reader follow the writer's thinking and arrangement of ideas?

- Are the grammar and spelling acceptable?

- Does the writer make positive changes in any or all of the above over the course of several drafts?

If these questions can increasingly be answered in the affirmative, then student writers are reaching the point of mainstream proficiency.

❖ EVALUATING READING

If you are expected to evaluate students' reading proficiency as well as their writing, we suggest the following steps:

1. For each student, select two or three reading cards from *The Multicultural Workshop Box* (described earlier). Choose readings that you and your colleagues think represent the level of difficulty your students should be capable of handling.

2. Ask students to choose the card they like best, read it, and write a "review" for their classmates. In their review, they should comment briefly on the contents of the reading and explain why and to whom it might be interesting.

3. Before students begin reading the card they have chosen, inform them of the criteria you will use to evaluate their work (see #5 below).

4. After students finish reading and writing, collect their reviews, keeping each review together with the reading card on which the review is based.

5. As you read the reviews, keep in mind the following questions:

   Does the student show that she/he can follow the reading?

   Does the student synthesize enough of the reading to be able to tell someone else about it? Does the student evaluate and analyze, as well as report?

   Does the student discern and select aspects of the reading that might interest classmates?

   Does the student bring her/his own views to bear on the reading? Are those views used to make sense of the reading and /or convey them to her/his classmates?

   Does the student relate relevant aspects of the reading to other readings?

   If you discern these complexities in students' responses to appropriately-difficult texts, then students are indeed becoming proficient and sophisticated readers.

❖ OTHER EVALUATION SCENARIOS

End-of-term evaluation procedures vary from program to program. While we think it ideal for students using *Writing Workshop* to be evaluated on the basis of their classwork, other scenarios may apply.

- In programs with portfolio assessment, the scenario is barely different from the one above for evaluating writing. Portfolios can be constructed as a "subset" of students' work in their writing folders. In a student's portfolio, we suggest including the following:

  1. two of the first seven workshop writing assignments, as selected by each writer on the basis of her/his best work

2. a writing test from workshop #8 (or a "mock" exam constructed by you)

3. a one- to two-page language/literacy autobiography (Written at the beginning of the academic term, it can serve as each student's introduction to his/her classmates. It can be revised later for the portfolio.)

4. a cover statement, explaining to evaluators the writer's choice of portfolio contents

- In programs in which proficiency exams determine grades and/or future placement, a student's writing folder, or a portfolio constructed from the folder, might be reviewed by an "appeals" committee, especially in cases where you know the exam results give a false reading of a student's proficiency.

- In programs in which results of proficiency exams are combined with students' coursework, the writing and/or reading evaluation scenarios detailed above may be used to determine course grade and future placement.

- In programs with competency-based assessment, the list of strategies on page ix can help determine the match between skills mandated by the curriculum and those employed by workshop students. In this scenario, an exam would need to be written by teachers using workshop materials to test the degree to which students can apply and use the strategies effectively.

Interpreting a Text

Many college writing assignments require students to interpret something they have read or seen. In this workshop, you will look at one person's interpretation of a movie and then write your own interpretation of a short story.

1. Group Work. What's the difference between describing and interpreting? Look at these signs and then answer the questions in the chart below.

⬛◆⬛◆⬛◆⬛◆⬛◆⬛◆

> **CRITICAL THINKING STRATEGY:**
> *021 Interpreting*
> See page 154.

a.

b.

c.

DESCRIBING **(What do you see?)**	**INTERPRETING** **(What does it mean to you?)**
a. *a wiggly arrow*	*the road curves ahead*
b. _____	_____
c. _____	_____

Get together with the other groups in your class and answer the questions below.

  a. Compare charts on page 1. How are your descriptions similar and different? What about your interpretations?

  b. Why might people from different cultures interpret these three things differently?

  c. What information did you need to interpret these three things?

  d. What's the difference between describing and interpreting?

2. On your own. Read the movie review on the next page and underline the ideas that describe what happened in the movie. Then read the review again and circle the sentences that give the writer's interpretation of the movie.

A scene from "The Garden of the Finzi-Continis," a Vittorio De Sica movie

The Garden of the Finzi-Continis: A Review

1   Until recently, the public could own memorable books but not memorable films. Videotape has changed all of that. So it was with great pleasure that I recently read of the re-release of Vittorio De Sica's 1971 film masterpiece, *The Garden of the Finzi-Continis.* I cannot wait to watch it again. Perhaps I will even buy my own copy.

2   Set in Ferrara, Italy, the film subconsciously reveals the brutality[1] of anti-Jewish sentiment,[2] policy, and procedures between the war years of 1938 and 1943. Consciously, what we view is the depiction[3] of an aristocratic Italian family living out the last moments of their doomed[4] lives.

3   As in any work of art, the messages found here are unavoidable truths. The truths of *The Finzi-Continis* concern stubbornness— both the stubbornness of the hateful heart and that of the hopeful heart.

4   One message of the film is that people often do not understand that their lives are doomed, especially when they live out their last days so seemingly normally. Another message is that one's grand estate[5] can, at the hands of a hateful state, become one's prison. As Mussolini's rule deepens,[6] the enchanted garden of the Finzi-Continis closes around them. Jews are banned from schools and libraries, from parks and offices. The Finzi-Continis have nowhere to be except their own home, where they continue to hope they will be safe from the outside world. Yet the high walls of their garden only hide the encroaching[7] evil on the other side. The ultimate truth of this film, then, is that the human heart blindly clings[8] to hope even in the face of certain destruction.

---

1 **brutality**   cruelty; a cruel and unfeeling action
2 **sentiment**   attitudes based on emotion, not reason
3 **depiction**   how something is shown or described
4 **doomed**   moving toward a tragic end
5 **estate**   a grand house surrounded by gardens and open land
6 **deepens**   becomes stronger
7 **encroaching**   advancing across others' rights, and threatening others' safety
8 **clings**   holds, hangs on

3. **Group Work.** Work together to answer the questions below.

    a. In Activity 2, did you circle and underline the same information? If not, see if you can agree on an answer.

    b. Match each paragraph in the review to one or more of the purposes below. Write the number of the paragraph.

CRITICAL THINKING
STRATEGY:
016 Analyzing
See page 144.

Purposes
_____   gives examples to support the writer's interpretation
_____   identifies the subject of the review
_____   gives the writer's interpretation of the movie
_____   tells what the movie is about

Compare ideas with the other groups in your class.

4. **On your own.** When you write about something you have read or seen, be sure to identify the subject of your writing. The sentences below show several ways to do this. Study the sentences and then choose a movie you have seen or a book you have read. On the lines on page 5, identify it in different ways.

- Vittorio De Sica's 1971 film, *The Garden of the Finzi-Continis*, has recently been re-released on video.

- *The Garden of the Finzi-Continis*, a 1971 film by Vittorio De Sica, has recently been re-released on video.

- The 1971 movie *The Garden of the Finzi-Continis*, by Vittorio De Sica, has recently been re-released on video.

- The book *Love in a Cold Climate*, by Nancy Mitford, tells the story of an eccentric family in England.

- Nancy Mitford's book *Love in a Cold Climate* is about an eccentric family in England.

- In her book *Love in a Cold Climate*, Nancy Mitford tells the story of an eccentric family in England.

- *Love in a Cold Climate*, a novel by Nancy Mitford, tells the story of an eccentric family in England.

_____

_____

_____

_____

_____

Read your ideas to the class.

5. **On your own.** Identifying reasons, messages, problems, or advantages is a common task in college writing. The example below shows one way to do this. Study the example and then complete the sentences below.

> **Example:**
>   One message of the film _The Garden of the Finzi-Continis_ <u>is</u> <u>that</u> people often do not understand that their lives are doomed, especially when they live out their last days so seemingly normally. <u>Another message is that</u> one's grand estate can, at the hands of a hateful state, become one's prison.

a. *(Choose a film you have seen.)* One message of the film _____

   _____

   is that _____

   _____ .

   Another message is that _____

   _____ .

b. One reason for studying English is that _____

   _____ .

   Another reason is that _____

   _____ .

c. One advantage of living in a city is that _____

_____ .

Another advantage is that _____

_____ .

d. One problem with wearing glasses is that _____

_____ .

Another problem is that _____

_____ .

Read your ideas to the class.

READING STRATEGY:
010 Previewing
See page 136.

6. **On your own.** In the next part of this workshop, you are going to read a short story and then write an interpretation of it. But before you read the story on page 7, preview it by completing the chart below.

1. **Title:** _____

2. **Author:** _____

3. **Genre:** ❑ **Fiction**   ❑ **Nonfiction**

4. **Level of difficulty:** ❑ **Easy**   ❑ **Challenging**   ❑ **Very challenging**

5. **What does the title make you think of? (List several things.)**

darkness

6. **Read the first two paragraphs of the story. What questions come to mind? (Think of two more questions.)**

What woke him up?

Compare charts with your classmates.

7. **On your own.** Writing down your thoughts and questions as you read helps you to read actively. As you read the story below, write your own thoughts and questions in the margin.

◨◇◨◨◨◇◨◨◨◇◨◨◨◇

READING STRATEGY:
015 Writing Margin Notes
See page 143.

Night

by Bret Lott

He woke up. He thought he could hear their child's breathing in the next room, the near-silent, smooth sound of air in and out.

He touched his wife. The room was too dark to let him see her, but he felt her movement, the shift of blanket and sheet.

"Listen," he whispered.

"Yesterday," she mumbled. "Why not yesterday," and she moved back into sleep.

He listened harder; though he could hear his wife's breath, thick and heavy next to him, there was beneath this the thin frost of his child's breathing.

The hardwood floor was cold beneath his feet. He held out a hand in front of him, and when he touched the doorjamb, he paused, listened again, heard the life in his child.

His fingertips led him along the hall and to the next room. Then he was in the doorway of a room as dark, as hollow as his own. He cut on the light.

The room, of course, was empty. They had left the bed just as their child had made it, the spread merely thrown over bunched and wrinkled sheets, the pillow crooked at the head. The small blue desk was littered with colored pencils and scraps of construction paper, a bottle of white glue.

He turned off the light and listened. He heard nothing, then backed out of the room and moved down the hall, back to his room, his hands at his sides, his fingertips helpless.

This happened each night, like a dream, but not.

▣◆▣□◇□▣□◆◘▣◇

READING STRATEGY:
014 Using Context
See page 140.

8. On your own. Choose five unfamiliar words or expressions from the story and add them to the chart below. First guess the meaning of each word, using context. Then look up the words in your dictionary to check your guesses.

Word	Word in context	My guess using context	Dictionary definition
mumbled	"Yesterday," she mumbled.	said slowly	to speak unclearly in a low voice

Get together with several classmates. Tell what you found out about these words.

▣◆▣□◇□▣□◆◘▣◇

READING STRATEGY:
011 Quickwriting
See page 136.

9. On your own. In your journal, quickwrite in response to the story "Night." Here are some questions to think about as you write:

a. What's the story about? Retell it briefly in your own words.

b. Why do you think the writer chose to call the story "Night"?

c. What issues does the story get you thinking about? What are the "messages" in this short story?

Get together with several classmates and share your responses to the questions.

10. **Writing Assignment.** Write a short review of the story on page 7. In the first paragraph, identify the story and briefly tell what it is about. Then, in one or more paragraphs, give and explain your interpretation of the story. Assume that your reader has not read the story.

WRITING STRATEGY:
003 Organizing Ideas
See page 119.

> ### Beginning
>
> Identify the subject of your interpretation and briefly tell what happens in the story.
>
> ### Middle
>
> Give your interpretation of the story. Give examples to support your interpretation.
>
> ### End
>
> Summarize your interpretation and leave your reader with something to think about.

11. **Pair Work.** Read your partner's review of the story and then answer the questions below.

CRITICAL THINKING STRATEGY:
020 Evaluating
See page 153.

	YES	NO
a. Does your partner identify the story by title and by author?	❏	❏
b. From the review, can you understand generally what the story is about?	❏	❏
c. Does your partner include no more information about the story than is necessary?	❏	❏
d. Does your partner give an interpretation of the story?	❏	❏
e. Does your partner give enough detail to explain the interpretation?	❏	❏

12. **On your own.** Using your classmate's evaluation from the activity above, write one or more revised drafts of your review. Then place them in your writing folder.

WRITING STRATEGY:
006 Revising
See page 124.

Grammar Workshop 1a: adjective clauses

1. **Read the examples in the box and then answer the questions that follow.**

   > *Examples*
   > - It's a story about a man **who decides to quit his job and go climb a mountain.**
   > - For people **who like to travel,** it's a great magazine.
   > - Music is the force **that has contributed most significantly to my development.**
   > - Through music, I can bring out feelings **that I cannot normally share.**
   > - Through music, I can bring out feelings **I cannot normally share.**

   a. The **boldfaced** words in each sentence form an adjective clause. What do you think the purpose of an adjective clause is?
   b. What words can you use to begin adjective clauses?
   c. When do you use "who"? When do you use "that"?
   d. When can you leave out the word "who" or "that"?
   e. The first example has a singular verb in the adjective clause. The second example has a plural verb. Why? *(Answers on page157.)*

2. **Underline the adjective clauses in these sentences.**

   a. There are several things that we could do to prevent children from smoking.
   b. One thing that confused me was the last line in the story.
   c. One dangerous thing that she did was to drive too fast.
   d. I learned how a friend I knew well could become my enemy.

3. **Think of a way to complete each sentence below.**

   a. I don't like movies that _____

   _____ .

   b. I prefer books that _____

   _____ .

   c. The story "Night" is about a father who _____

   _____ .

   d. It's important for children to read books that _____

   _____ .

   e. In the story "Night," a father gets up and goes to a room that _____

   _____ .

Grammar Workshop 1b: appositives

1. Read the examples in the box and then answer the questions that follow.

> *Examples*
> - The story "Night" is from *A Dream of Old Leaves,* **a collection of short stories by Bret Lott.**
> - *The Garden of the Finzi-Continis,* **a movie by Vittorio De Sica,** was filmed in Italy.
> - I'd like to see other movies by the director **Vittorio De Sica.**

a. We call the group of **boldfaced** words in each sentence above an "appositive." What do you think the purpose of an appositive is?

b. In the third sentence in the box, the writer didn't use a comma before or after the appositive. Why? How is this appositive different from the others? *(Answers on page 158.)*

2. Underline the appositive in each sentence below. Then add commas where needed.

a. In Brazil Latin America's largest country President Getúlio Vargas came to power in 1934.

b. Followers of Mohandas Gandhi leader of the Indian independence movement used nonviolent methods to protest British administration of their country.

c. In the early 1970s, American scientists and engineers developed the space shuttle a reusable spacecraft that could take off like a rocket.

d. In March 1979, Anwar el-Sadat and Menachem Begin signed a peace treaty the first ever signed between an Arab nation and Israel.

e. In the 1920s, the Irish writer James Joyce found a publisher for his novel *Ulysses* an account of a day in the lives of three ordinary people in Dublin, Ireland.

3. Add more information to each sentence below, using the words in parentheses. Rewrite each sentence and include commas when necessary. The first one is done for you.

a. (the first electronic computer)
ENIAC weighed 30 tons and could do only 5000 calculations per second.

ENIAC, the first electronic computer, weighed 30 tons and could do only 5000 calculations

per second.

b. ("Guernica")
   Picasso painted his famous antiwar painting after the bombing of the village of Guernica.

   _____

   _____ .

c. (a play dealing with his country's freedom)
   In 1963 the Nigerian playwright Wole Soyinka wrote "A Dance of the Forests."

   _____

   _____ .

d. (a book that tried to summarize all medical knowledge)
   Doctor Ibn Sina wrote "The Canon of Medicine" in the 800s.

   _____

   _____ .

e. (a Scottish engineer)
   The first working television system was developed in 1926 by John Baird.

   _____

   _____ .

f. (the designer of the Vietnam Memorial in Washinton, D.C.)
   Maya Lin was, at the time, a student of architecture at Yale University.

   _____

   _____ .

g. (a Moghul emperor) (Mumtaz Mahal)
   The Taj Mahal was built in the 1640s by Shah Jahan as a memorial to his wife.

   _____

   _____ .

Summarizing Nonfiction

*Summarizing is involved in many kinds of college
writing assignments. In this workshop, you will read a
magazine article and then evaluate several summaries
of the article. Finally, you will choose an article of
interest to you and write a brief summary of it.*

1. **On your own.** Which of these types of nonfiction have you read
   this month? Check (✔) your answers.

   ❏ a newspaper article

   ❏ a magazine article

   ❏ a chapter from a biography

   ❏ an essay

   ❏ a chapter from an autobiography

   ❏ a chapter from a textbook

   ❏ a scientific report

   ❏ an obituary

   Compare answers with your classmates.

The health plan that's best for your neighbor may not be best for you. A guide to finding one that meets your needs.

THERE'S A DIRTY LITTLE SECRET that nobody tells you when it comes time to pluck a health-care plan from your employer's benefits package. Most health-maintenance organizations are good at some things—and others. Is an HMO heart care th...

Afterword: A Look Back at Ethnographic Research

To those who have read the . . . preceding chapters, the data and findings of this study may well appear self-evident. It may seem that all I had to do was spend enough time . . . to learn—inevitably and unavoid-... that I finally learned. In fact, that may seem to ... any ethnographic study when encoun-... form. Yet that is not the reality ... Fishman,

Jazz club loses bid for landma[rk]

By Mark A. Brunelli
GLOBE CORRESPONDENT

A three-year crusade to grant landmark status to Connolly's Tavern, a historic jazz club on Tremont Street in Roxbury, failed this week and area residents may soon see a new supermarket in its place.

Despite acknowledging its cultural significance in Boston's jazz history, the city's nine-member Landmarks Commission, which ed on the issue T...

chairman Alan G. Schwartz said that even if proponents got the two-thirds majority, the club itself would not have been saved since the building's owners, the Boston Redevelopment Authority, have already sent a notice of eviction to its tenants. The building was erected in 1882.

Kelley Quinn, a spokeswoman for the BRA, said Roxbury overwhelming...

1965, patro... could swing drummer To... ist Zoot Sim... Roy Eldridge.

Schwartz s... Commission and tiating an ...

READING STRATEGY:
010 Previewing
See page 136.

2. **On your own.** Preview the piece of nonfiction on pages 15–18 and complete the chart below.

1. Title: _____

2. Author: _____

3. Level of difficulty: ❏ Easy ❏ Challenging ❏ Very challenging

4. What does the title make you think of?

5. Based on the title, what do you think the essay is about?

6. Scan the essay. Do any words stand out? What do you think the essay is about?

3. On your own. Read the essay below several times and write your thoughts and questions in the margin.

◻◈◻◈◻◈◻◈◻◻

READING STRATEGY:
*015 Writing Margin
Notes*
See page 143.

Friends, Good Friends—And Such Good Friends
by Judith Viorst

Women are friends, I once would have said, when they totally love and support and trust each other, and bare to each other the secrets of their souls, and run—no questions asked—to help each other, and tell harsh truths to each other ("no, you can't wear that dress unless you lose ten pounds first") when harsh truths must be told.

Women are friends, I once would have said, when they share the same affection for Ingmar Bergman, plus train rides, cats, warm rain, charades,[1] Camus, and hate with equal ardor[2] Newark and Brussells sprouts and Lawrence Welk and camping.

In other words, I once would have said that a friend is a friend all the way,[3] but now I believe that's a narrow point of view.[4] For the friendships I have and the friendships I see are conducted at many levels of intensity, serve many different functions, meet different needs and range from those as all-the-way as the friendship of the soul sisters[5] mentioned above to that of the most nonchalant and casual playmates.

Consider these varieties of friendship:

1. **Convenience friends.** These are the women with whom, if our paths weren't crossing[6] all the time, we'd have no particular reason to be friends: a next-door neighbor, a woman in our car pool, the mother of one of our children's closest friends or maybe some mommy with whom we serve juice and cookies each week at the Glenwood Co-op Nursery.

   Convenience friends are convenient indeed. They'll lend us their cups and silverware for a party. They'll drive our

---

1 **charades**   games in which words are acted out
2 **with equal ardor**   with the same strength
3 **all the way**   completely; totally
4 **a narrow point of view**   an incomplete way of seeing something
5 **soul sisters**   unrelated women who are very alike emotionally, spiritually, etc.
6 **if our paths weren't crossing**   if we didn't see each other

kids to soccer when we're sick. They'll take us to pick up our car when we need a lift[7] to the garage. They'll even take our cats when we go on vacation. As we will for them.

But we don't, with convenience friends, ever come too close[8] or tell too much; we maintain our public face and emotional distance. "Which means," says Elaine, "that I'll talk about being overweight but not about being depressed. Which means I'll admit being mad but not blind with rage.[9] Which means I might say that we're pinched[10] this month but never that I'm worried sick over money."

But which doesn't mean that there isn't sufficient value to be found in these friendships of mutual aid, in convenience friends.

2. **Special-interest friends.** These friendships aren't intimate, and they needn't involve kids or silverware or cats. Their value lies in some interest jointly shared. And so we may have an office friend or a yoga friend or a tennis friend or a friend from the Women's Democratic Club.

"I've got one woman friend, says Joyce, "who likes, as I do, to take psychology courses. Which makes it nice for me—and nice for her. It's fun to go with someone you know and it's fun to discuss what you've learned, driving back from the classes." And for the most part, she says, that's all they discuss.

"I'd say that what we're doing is *doing* together, not being together," Suzanne says of her Tuesday-doubles friends.[11] "It's mainly a tennis relationship, but we play together well. And I guess we all need to have a couple of playmates."

I agree.

My playmate is a shopping friend, a woman of marvelous taste, a woman who knows exactly *where* to buy *what*, and

---

7 **a lift**   a ride by car
8 **come too close**   become very intimate
9 **blind with rage**   extremely angry
10 **pinched**   short of money; without extra money
11 **Tuesday-doubles friends**   friends she plays doubles tennis with on Tuesday

16

furthermore is a woman who always knows beyond a doubt what one *ought* to be buying. I don't have the time to keep up with what's new in eyeshadow, hemlines and shoes and whether the smock look is in[12] or finished already. But since (oh, shame!) I care a lot about eyeshadow, hemlines and shoes, and since I don't *want* to wear smocks if the smock look is finished, I'm very glad to have a shopping friend.

3. **Historical friends.** We all have a friend who knew us when…maybe way back in Miss Meltzer's second grade, when our family lived in that three-room flat in Brooklyn, when our dad was out of work for seven months, when our brother Allie got in that fight where they had to call the police, when our sister married the endodontist from Yonkers…

   The years have gone by and we've gone separate ways and we've little in common now, but we're still an intimate part of each other's past. And so whenever we go to Detroit we always go to visit this friend of our girlhood. Who knows how we talked before our voice got *un*Brooklyned. Who knows what we ate before we learned about artichokes. And who, by her presence, puts us in touch[13] with an earlier part of ourselves, a part of ourselves it's important never to lose.

   "What this friend means to me and what I mean to her," says Grace, "is having a sister without sibling rivalry.[14] We know the texture of each other's lives. She remembers my grandmother's cabbage soup. I remember the way her uncle played the piano. There's simply no other friend who remembers those things.

4. **Crossroad friends.** Like historical friends, our crossroad friends are important for *what was*—for the friendship we shared at a crucial, now past, time of life. A time, perhaps, when we roomed in college together; or worked as eager young singles in the Big City together; or went together, as

---

12 **is in** is popular
13 **puts us in touch with** reminds us of; makes us remember
14 **sibling rivalry** competition among the children in one family

my friend Elizabeth and I did through pregnancy, birth and that scary first year of new motherhood.

Crossroad friends forge powerful links, links strong enough to endure with not much more contact than once-a-year letters at Christmas. And out of respect for those crossroads years, for those dramas and dreams we once shared, we will always be friends…

5. There are medium friends, and pretty good friends, and very good friends indeed, and these friendships are defined by their level of intimacy. And what we'll reveal at each of these levels of intimacy is calibrated with care. We might tell a medium friend, for example, that yesterday we had a fight with our husband. And we might tell a pretty good friend that this fight with our husband made us so mad that we slept on the couch. And we might tell a very good friend that the reason we got so mad in that fight that we slept on the couch had something to do with that girl who works in his office. But it's only to our very best friends that we're willing to tell all, to tell what's going on with that girl in his office.

The best of friends, I still believe, totally love and support and trust each other, and bare to each other the secrets of their souls, and run—no questions asked—to help each other, and tell harsh truths to each other when they must be told.

But we needn't agree about everything (only 12-year-old girl-friends agree about *everything)* to tolerate each other's point of view. To accept without judgment. To give and to take without ever keeping score. And to *be* there, as I am for them and as they are for me, to comfort our sorrows, to celebrate our joys.

READING STRATEGY:
014 Using Context
See page 140.

4. **On your own.** Choose five unfamiliar words or expressions from the story and add them to the chart on the next page. First guess the meaning of each word, using context. Then look up the words in your dictionary to check your guesses.

Word	Word in context	My guess using context	Dictionary definition
bare	"and bare to each other the secrets of their souls"	tell	to show, to expose

Get together with several classmates. Tell what you learned about these words.

5. **Pair Work.** Read the definition below and then answer the questions that follow.

> "Thesis statements introduce the theme of the whole piece of writing. If papers are written in answer to questions—implied or explicit—it is the thesis that announces the direction that the answer will take."
>
> from *College Writing* by Toby Fulwiler

WRITING STRATEGY:
002 Making Your Thesis Clear
See page 117.

a. Look back at the essay on pages 15–18. Does it have a thesis statement? If so, what is it?

b. A piece of academic writing often has a thesis statement. Why do you think this is so?

Compare ideas with your classmates.

CRITICAL THINKING
STRATEGY
016 Analyzing
See page 144.

WRITING STRATEGY:
007 Summarizing
See page 128.

6. **Group Work.** Work together to answer the questions below. Then report your answers to the class.

   a. Who do you think Viorst wrote this essay for? How would you describe her audience? Do you consider yourself a member of this audience?

   b. What do you think Viorst's purpose is in this essay? In other words, what do you think she hopes to achieve?

   c. How would you characterize Viorst's style of writing? Formal? Businesslike? Casual? Find examples to illustrate your answer.

7. **On your own.** In the next part of this workshop, you will look at how to write a summary of something you have read. To begin, look at page 128 of the Reference Guide to find three characteristics of a summary. List them below.

   _____

   _____

   _____

   Share ideas with your classmates.

8. **Group Work.** Read the paragraph below from the Viorst essay and a summary of it. Then read the statements that follow and check (✔) YES or NO.

   Original paragraph from the Viorst essay:

   "There are medium friends, and pretty good friends, and very good friends indeed, and these friendships are defined by their level of intimacy. And what we'll reveal at each of these levels of intimacy is calibrated with care. We might tell a medium friend, for example, that yesterday we had a fight with our husband. And we might tell a pretty good friend that this fight with our husband made us so mad that we slept on the couch. And we might tell a very good friend that the reason we got so mad in that fight that we slept on the couch had something to do with that girl who works in his office. But it's only to our very best friends that we're willing to tell all, to tell what's going on with that girl in his office."

Summary:

According to Viorst, friendships can be categorized by their "level of intimacy" or by how much personal information we are willing to reveal.

	YES	NO
a. The summary is much shorter than the original.	❑	❑
b. The summary provides lots of details.	❑	❑
c. The summary states only the main idea of the original.	❑	❑

Share ideas with your classmates.

9. **Group Work.** Read the paragraph from Viorst's essay below and the three summaries of it. Then answer the questions that follow.

Original paragraph from the Viorst essay:

"In other words, I once would have said that a friend is a friend all the way, but now I believe that's a narrow point of view. For the friendships I have and the friendships I see are conducted at many levels of intensity, serve many different functions, meet different needs and range from those as all-the-way as the friendship of the soul sisters mentioned above to that of the most nonchalant and casual playmates."

Summary #1

According to Viorst, there are many different kinds of friendship with varying levels of intensity.

Summary #2

According to Viorst, it's a narrow point of view to say that a friend is a friend all the way because friendships are conducted at many levels of intensity, serve different functions, and meet different needs.

Summary #3

According to Viorst, there are many different kinds of friendship, ranging from soul sisters to casual playmates.

a. Which words from the original paragraph does each summary writer use? Circle them.

b. When you write a summary, it's important to "use your own words." Which of the three summary writers used her own words? Why do you think so?

c. What exactly does it mean to "use your own words"? Can you use *any* words from the original article?

Share ideas with the other groups in your class.

10. **On your own.** Use your own words to briefly define each of Viorst's terms below.

a. a convenience friend

_____

_____

_____

b. a special interest friend

_____

_____

_____

c. a crossroad friend

_____

_____

_____

Get together with several classmates and compare ideas.

11. **Pair Work.** Below are two summaries of the Viorst article on pages 15–18. Read both summaries and answer these questions.

   a. How are the two summaries different?

   b. Which summary shows a better understanding of the orignal article? Why?

   c. Which summary is clearer to you? Why?

   d. What would you do to improve each summary? Make a specific suggestion.

   e. Did the writers use their own words? Give examples to support your answer.

CRITICAL THINKING STRATEGY:
020 Evaluating
See page 153.

Summary #1

In her essay, entitled "Friends, Good Friends—And Such Good Friends," Judith Viorst writes about friendships from a broad viewpoint. Classifying friendships by their many levels of intensity and different functions, she comes up with these categories: convenience friends, special-interest friends, historical friends, crossroads friends, and friends defined by different levels of intimacy.

Summary #2

Judith Viorst wrote an essay about friends. She says that the friendships she has "are conducted at many levels of intensity, serve many different functions, and meet different needs." Her convenience friends are ones she crosses paths with. She wouldn't be friends with them if they weren't convenient. The value of her special-interest friends lies in a jointly shared interest. Her historical friends are friends who remember things from the past, like what happened when she was in elementary school. Her crossroad friends are important for the friendship they shared. Finally, some of her friendships can be defined by her level of intimacy with them: medium friends, pretty good friends, and very good friends. Viorst says that "The best of friends…totally love and support and trust each other."

Share ideas with your classmates.

23

CRITICAL THINKING
STRATEGY:
020 Evaluating
See page 153.

12. Pair Work. Evaluate the two summaries on page 23. Check (✔) the statements that describe each one.

	Summary #1 YES	Summary #1 NO	Summary #2 YES	Summary #2 NO
a. Does the writer of the summary identify the original article?	❏	❏	❏	❏
b. Does the writer use her own words?	❏	❏	❏	❏
c. Is the summary clear?	❏	❏	❏	❏
d. Does the writer do more than simply report information?	❏	❏	❏	❏

13. Writing Assignment. Choose a short piece of nonfiction that interests you and follow the steps below to write a summary of it.

a. Make a copy of the article or essay to hand in with your summary.

b. Preview the article before you read it.

c. Read it several times. Write your thoughts and questions in the margin. Underline the writer's main ideas. Become thoroughly familiar with the article.

d. In your own words, answer these questions:

• What's the writer's main point?

• What are the most important things that the writer wants me to understand?

e. Look over your notes and think about how you might organize your ideas. Then write a first draft of your summary.

f. Ask a classmate to evaluate your summary, using the questions in Activity 12.

g. Working from your classmate's evaluation, write several more drafts of your summary and place them in your writing folder.

WRITING STRATEGY:
006 Revising
See page 124.

Grammar Workshop 2a: noun clauses with "that"

1. **Read the examples in the box and then answer the questions that follow.**

> *Examples*
> - In her essay, Judith Viorst suggests **that there are many different kinds of friendship.**
> - In his speech last night, the President said **that he had decided not to run for office again.**
> - I think **that Viorst's essay is very interesting.**
> - I think **Viorst's essay is very interesting.**
> - People used to think **that the world was flat.**
> - People used to think **the world was flat.**

  a. The **boldfaced** words in each sentence form a noun clause. What is the subject and verb in each noun clause? What is the subject and verb in each main clause?

  b. What is the purpose of the noun clause in the first example?

  c. Is it possible to omit the word "that" in the first example in the box? *(Answers on page 158.)*

2. **Complete these sentences.**

  a. I think that friends _____.

  b. In the movie review on page 3, the writer claims that _____

  _____.

  c. In her essay, Judith Viorst argues that _____

  _____.

  d. People used to think that _____

  _____.

  e. I believe that students _____

  _____.

3. **Now add a noun clause to complete each of these sentences.**

  a. I used to think _____ but I don't anymore.

  b. When you travel to a foreign country, I suggest _____

  _____.

Grammar Workshop 2b: reported speech

1. **Read the examples in the box and then answer the questions that follow.**

> *Examples*
>
> - In her essay, Viorst **says** that some friendships **are** less intimate than others.
>
> - In *The Declaration of Independence,* Thomas Jefferson **says** that all men **are** equal.
>
> - In his autobiography, *My Experiments with Truth,* Mohandas Gandhi **argues** that truth **is** achievable through love and tolerance for other people.
>
> - Thomas Jefferson **said** that all men **are** equal.
>
> - Mohandas Gandhi (1869–1948) **said** that it **is** difficult but not impossible to be an honest business person.

   a. In the sentences above, the writer is reporting what someone else said or wrote. In each sentence she uses a present tense verb in the noun clause. Why do you think she does this?

   b. In the first three examples, the writer uses a present tense verb in the main clause. In examples 4 and 5, the writer uses a past tense verb in the main clause. Why do you think she does this? *(Answers on page 158.)*

2. **Complete each sentence with the correct verb in parentheses.**

   a. In her essay, Judith Viorst _____ that there are many different kinds of friendship.

   (argues / argued)

   b. In her essay about friends, Viorst _____ that her understanding of friendship has

   changed. (claims / claimed)

3. **The verbs below are often followed by a noun clause beginning with "that." Write sentences using three of these words to tell about something in the Viorst essay. Remember to use your own words.**

admit	explain	point out
argue	insist	say
claim	mention	suggest

Writing in Response to Reading

In your college coursework, you may be asked to read an article and answer a question about it in writing. In this workshop, you will have the chance to read sample responses to questions and then write your own response to a text-based question.

1. **Class Work.** After reading a text like the Viorst essay on pages 15–18, you might be asked to answer a question about it in writing. Below are some typical questions you could be asked. Identify each type of question.

R = asks you to **report** on what you read
I = asks you to **interpret** or **analyze** what you read

_R___   a. What is Viorst's definition of friendship?

_____   b. Do you agree with Viorst's definition of friendship?

_____   c. Do you accept all of Viorst's categories of friendship? Which categories seem the most meaningful to you?

_____   d. According to Viorst, what are convenience friends?

_____   e. In your own words, describe the different types of friendship that Viorst identifies.

_____   f. Does Viorst emphasize each of her categories of friendship equally?

_____   g. How does Viorst organize her ideas about friendship?

WRITING STRATEGY:
004 Paraphrasing
See page 121.

2. On your own. When you answer a question about a text, you may want to quote or paraphrase the writer of the text. What is the difference between quoting and paraphrasing? Look on page 122 of the Reference Guide and then list two differences on the lines below.

a. _____

_____

b. _____

_____

Compare ideas with your classmates.

WRITING STRATEGY:
004 Paraphrasing
See page 121.

3. On your own. When you include someone else's ideas in your writing, you can use a direct quotation or a paraphrase. In the sentences below, the writer chose to quote Judith Viorst. Rewrite these sentences, paraphrasing Viorst. Be sure to use your own words and to identify the source of the idea. The first one is done for you.

a. Direct Quotation: In her article, Viorst states that convenience friends are "the women with whom, if our paths weren't crossing all the time, we'd have no particular reason to be friends."

   Paraphrase: According to Viorst, "convenience friends" are the women who we consider friends solely because we see them frequently.

b. Direct Quotation: According to Viorst, crossroad friends "are important for what was—for the friendship we shared at a crucial, now past, time of life."

   Paraphrase: _____

_____

_____

_____

_____

_____

c. Direct Quotation: In her article "Friends, Good Friends—And Such Good Friends," Judith Viorst writes, "There are medium friends, and pretty good friends, and very good friends indeed, and these friendships are defined by their level of intimacy."

Paraphrase:

    _____

    _____

    _____

    _____

    _____

    _____

d. Direct Quotation: According to Viorst, some people are her friends because of "the friendship we shared at a crucial, now past, time of life."

Paraphrase:

    _____

    _____

    _____

    _____

    _____

    _____

Compare ideas with your classmates.

Writing Workshop

CRITICAL THINKING STRATEGY: 016 Analyzing See page 144.

4. **Pair Work.** Read two writers' responses to the text-based question below. Then answer the questions that follow.

What is Viorst's definition of friendship?

Writer #1

In her essay "Friends, Good Friends—And Such Good Friends," Judith Viorst maintains that there is no single definition of friendship. To prove this, she looks at the friendships in her life and shows how they can be classified into different categories. For example, Viorst claims that some of her friendships are based solely on convenience while others are based on a shared interest or a shared experience in the past. Although the level of intimacy is different in each type of relationship, for Viorst they are all examples of friendship.

Writer #2

There are many different kinds of friendship. Some friendships are very intimate. People in this type of friendship totally love and support and trust each other. They bare to each other the secrets of their souls. Some friendships are based solely on convenience. These are people you wouldn't be friends with if your paths weren't crossing all the time. These convenience friends don't ever come too close or tell too much. They maintain their public face and emotional distance.

a. One writer doesn't really answer the question. Which one?

b. Which writer is not using his own words? Give an example to support your answer.

c. Which answer makes a connection to the question? How might this be helpful to the reader?

d. Which answer do you think is better? Why?

Share your answers with your classmates.

CRITICAL THINKING STRATEGY: 019 Comparing See page 150.

5. **Group Work.** Read one writer's response to another text-based question. Then work together to tell how this response is different from the responses in Activity 4.

30

Do you agree with Viorst's definition of friendship?

In her essay "Friends, Good Friends—And Such Good Friends," Judith Viorst maintains that there is no single definition of friendship. To prove this, she looks at the friendships in her life and shows how they can be grouped into different categories. For example, Viorst claims that some of her friendships are based solely on convenience. Other friendships are based on a shared interest or a shared experience in the past. While the level of intimacy between people in each category of friendship may vary, in Viorst's opinion, they are all examples of friendship.

Like Viorst, I think that there are many different types of friendship. I have some friends to whom I am very close and for whom I would do anything. But I also have friends I care about and like to do things with but with whom I am not very intimate. They are all friends, just different kinds of friends.

Share ideas with the other groups in your class.

6. **Group Work.** A "writing prompt" is different from a direct question about a text. A writing prompt is designed to help you come up with your own writing topic. Read this prompt and then answer the questions below.

Writing Prompt

Try to think of people you know who fit into the various categories established by Viorst. Can you think of people who might exist in more than one category? How do you explain this fact? What are the dangers in trying to stereotype people in terms of categories, roles, backgrounds, or functions?

from *The Short Prose Reader*

a. Does the prompt instruct you to write only about Viorst's essay?

b. Which part of the prompt comes closest to instructing you about a topic for your own writing?

c. What purpose is served by asking a yes/no question?

d. In responding to this prompt, how much attention should you pay to Viorst?

◨◇◧◙◯◇◙◯◇◧◯◨

READING STRATEGY:
*015 Writing Margin
Notes*
See page 143.

7. On your own. Below is one student's response to the writing prompt in Activity 6. Read this essay and write your ideas and questions in the margin.

Friends

The dangers of categorizing one's friends outweigh any possible benefits this task might hold. It seems hard to believe that someone could easily sit down and catalogue her friends, as Judith Viorst has done in her essay "Friends, Good Friends—And Such Good Friends." Dividing friends into categories and sub-categories assigns a sort of judgment value to them. It's like saying, "Well, I only shop and play tennis with Mary. Do I know her well enough to tell her she's about to be hit by a truck?"

People should value friendship, but not in a "chopped liver versus steak" sort of way. If the world functioned according to strict categories of friends, it would run amuck. People would have to carry around long lists to remember which friends fit into which categories. People would have to sit at home making graphs and pie-charts to determine which friend was the best friend, the close friend, the convenience friend, etc. Dividing friends into groups is a useless task because friends constantly overlap and drop into and out of any group a person may put them in. Someone who is your friend of convenience today could be your best friend next week. Similarly, your best friend today could be at the bottom of your list tomorrow.

My best friend through college was someone I met when we were both thirteen. When we first met, I didn't like her very much. I thought she was snotty and uptight. But as time passed, I realized she was kind of nice. I could borrow class notes from her if I had missed a class or catch a ride home if I missed the bus. By the end of high school, we were going out on the weekends, double-dating at prom, and planning to be roommates in college. Once we had graduated from high school, we were best friends. By the time we set foot in the college dormitory, we were inseparable. We told

32

each other our deepest secrets and eventually moved into our first apartment together. We reached the peak of our friendship six years after we met.

Now I've moved far away, and I find myself not turning to thoughts of her as often. Living in a new city, I have met a new group of people, and our friendships have developed to various degrees, just as my friendships from high school did. I have met people with whom I don't have a really close friendship and people who function above and beyond the call of friendship. Nonetheless, they are all people I call my friends.

When I go to visit my friend from college or she comes to visit me, it is as if we never separated. We can talk about anything or nothing. We can argue or laugh. Even though we see each other maybe only twice a year and live 1500 miles apart, she hasn't dropped to some sub-standard level of friendship. She is simply my friend. Dividing my friends into groups would do nothing but cause aggravation and trivialize their importance. Friends are friends.

—*Jennifer A. Kuchta*
Student, University of New Orleans

---

8. **Group Work.** Work together to evaluate the essay in Activity 7.

   a. Does it have a thesis? If so, what is it?

   b. Why does she cite Viorst in the first paragraph?

   c. How much of the essay is about Viorst's ideas? How much is about the writer's own ideas?

   d. What is this writer arguing? Is she persuasive?

   e. What, if anything, is unclear to you in this essay?

   Share ideas with your classmates.

CRITICAL THINKING STRATEGY:
020 Evaluating
See page 153.

9. Writing Assignment. Follow the steps below to respond in writing to this prompt.

> **Writing Prompt**
>
> Viorst maintains that you can define friends in terms of functions and needs. Do you agree? Why or why not? What principle or principles do *you* use to classify friends? In fact, do you classify friends? For what reasons?
>
> from *The Short Prose Reader*

a. What are you going to write about? Explore your ideas by quick-writing for five to ten minutes in response to the questions in the writing prompt.

b. Reread your quickwriting. Look for an idea that you can develop into a one- to two-page essay.

c. Decide on your thesis. Then test your thesis by completing the chart below.

WRITING STRATEGY:
005 Quickwriting
See page 123.

WRITING STRATEGY:
002 Making Your Thesis Clear
See page 117.

Thesis: _____

_____

_____

Supporting Ideas

_____

_____

_____

_____

_____

_____

If this thesis doesn't work out, try another one.

d. Think about how you might organize your ideas in writing. Try answering the questions in the chart below.

WRITING STRATEGY:
003 Organizing Ideas
See page 119.

Beginning

What can I say to get my reader's interest?
How do I want to introduce my thesis?

Middle

What points do I want to make to support my thesis? Which point should I make first? Next? How much detail should I provide?

End

How can I end my writing? What interesting thought can I leave my reader with? What do I want my reader to be thinking about when he or she finishes my essay?

e. Write a first draft of your paper.

f. Exchange essays with a partner. Use the chart below to evaluate your partner's writing.

CRITICAL THINKING STRATEGY:
020 Evaluating
See page 153.

	YES
• Is the topic limited enough?	❏
• Does the introduction guide the reader?	❏
• Can the reader perceive the writer's plan?	❏
• Are the ideas connected?	❏
• Does the writer's voice come through?	❏

Share your evaluation with your partner. Listen to your partner's ideas about your essay.

WRITING STRATEGY:
006 Revising
See page 124.

g. Write one or more drafts of your essay and then place your writing in your writing folder.

Grammar Workshop 3a: *it's* + adjective + infinitive

1. Read the examples in the box. Then think of another way to complete the sentences that follow.

> *Examples*
> - **It's hard to believe** that someone could sit down and catalogue her friends.
> - **It's not unusual to feel** nervous before you take an exam or give a speech.
> - I think **it's crazy to spend** your life watching TV.
> - **It's strange** for someone **to leave** without saying goodbye.

a. It's hard to believe _____

_____ .

b. It's not unusual to feel _____

_____ .

c. I think it's crazy to spend _____

_____ .

d. It's strange for someone to leave _____

_____ .

2. Choose an adjective to complete each sentence below. More than one answer is possible.

a. Most people think it's _____ to steal.

b. When I was young, it was _____ for children to walk to school.

c. I don't understand why some people think it's _____ to smoke.

d. Judith Viorst thinks that it's _____ to have different kinds of friends.

3. **Give your opinion about each activity below. In your sentence, try to use** *it's* **+ adjective + infinitive. The first one is done for you.**

  a. (study a foreign language)

    It's important to study a foreign language, especially if you want to travel or work in international business.

  b. (wear appropriate clothing)

    _____

    _____

  c. (be patient)

    _____

    _____

  d. (take care of)

    _____

    _____

  e. (cheat on an exam)

    _____

    _____

  f. (buy car insurance)

    _____

    _____

Grammar Workshop 3b: gerunds as subjects

1. Read the examples in the box and then answer the questions that follow.

> **Examples**
>
> • Dividing friends into categories assigns a sort of judgment value to them.
>
> • Focusing your topic is one of the most important steps in writing an essay.
>
> • Growing up as immigrants in a new country can be confusing for children.

a. What's the subject of each sentence? What's the main verb?

b. Why might a writer choose to begin a sentence with a gerund? *(Answers on page 159.)*

2. Complete these sentences. The first one is done for you.

a. Reading extensively *is a good way to expand your vocabulary.* _____

b. Proofreading your writing _____.

c. Writing several drafts of a paper _____.

d. Writing margin notes as you read_____.

3. Change the focus of each sentence below by using a gerund as the subject.

a. It's important to understand the writing prompt before you write your first draft of an essay.

_____

_____

b. It's often useful to quickwrite when you need to collect ideas for an essay.

_____

_____

d. Most doctors say that it is good for you to eat a lot of fruit and vegetables.

_____

_____

Incorporating Others' Ideas Into Your Writing

In college courses, you will be expected to incorporate others' ideas and research into your writing. How do you do this? In this workshop, you will learn to cite or document sources, report on research, and evaluate new ideas, all within the framework of your own thinking.

1. **On your own.** Look over the magazine article on pages 40–44 and complete the chart below.

READING STRATEGY:
010 Previewing
See page 136.

1. Title: _____

2. Author: _____

3. Genre: ❏ Fiction   ❏ Nonfiction

4. Level of difficulty: ❏ Easy   ❏ Challenging   ❏ Very challenging

5. What does the title make you think of? What questions does it raise for you?

6. Read the first sentence in each paragraph. What do you think the article is about?

Compare charts with your classmates.

READING STRATEGY:
015 Writing Margin Notes
See page 143.

2. **Group Work.** The article below begins with a question. Before reading, answer the question and share your answer with your classmates.

3. **On your own.** Read the article several times and write notes in the margin. Then share your notes with a partner.

7 Keys to Learning

Phyllis La Farge

When you think of people whom you would describe as intelligent, who comes to mind?[1] The boy in grade school who always had the right answers to math problems? The mechanic who pinpointed trouble in your car? The new manager at work who restructured your department? The friend who seems to understand what's on your mind almost before you do? Your child, who wrote a beautiful poem when your family dog died? The girl with the highest SAT[2] score in your high school class?

Indeed, all of these individuals are smart—but in different ways. That's the idea behind the theory of intelligence proposed by Howard Gardner, Ph.D.—codirector of Harvard University's Project Zero, and a professor of education at the Harvard Graduate School of Education—that is being applied in schools throughout the nation.

Rather than a single, generalized ability called "intelligence" that can be described by an IQ score,[3] Gardner believes that we have multiple intelligences (MIs)—although we are probably not equally well endowed in all of them—and that these intelligences are not restricted to the two cognitive[4] areas of words and numbers, the ones most likely to be rec-

---

Musical

Sensitivity to what Howard Gardner, Ph.D., calls the "principal constituent elements" of music: pitch or melody, rhythm, and timbre or quality of tone.
Adult roles: Discriminating music listener, performer, composer, conductor, music critic.

Signs of promise in the 5- or 6-year-old: Being able to sing in key, keep a beat, compose his own songs, and remember music that he has heard. Musical talent is one of the earliest to emerge.

---

1 **who comes to mind?** who do you think of?
2 **SAT** Scholastic Aptitude Test, a test taken by students for college admission
3 **IQ score** results of a test that supposedly measures your intelligence
4 **cognitive** referring to the workings of the brain

Interpersonal

The ability to notice distinctions among people and, particularly, to perceive their "moods, temperaments, motivations, and intentions."

Adult roles: Teacher, salesperson, politician, community organizer, therapist, religious leader.

Signs of promise in the 5- or 6-year-old: Has friends and enjoys group activities; if the child is more detached, still knows who plays with whom; displays empathy.

---

ognized and rewarded when children start school.

For instance, ever since she was a toddler, 5-year-old Amy has had excellent powers of concentration. She is a wonderful observer; her parents have seen her watch a bug for minutes at a time and draw a caterpillar from memory. Yet her teacher has told them that Amy does not stay "on task"[5] and has started to be a behavior problem.[6]

Or take Sam, who is 6 and in first grade. He is having a hard time learning to read, yet his parents know that in certain ways he is gifted.[7] He is skilled and inventive with construction toys; and the other day, when his mother got out the old-fashioned meat grinder that she still uses, he offered to put it together—and succeeded on the first try.

Children like Amy and Sam are certainly as smart as other kindergartners and first-graders who catch on[8] quickly to reading and math. Gardner points out that our culture values some human abilities at the expense of others and that, as a result, we often fail to develop our children's potential. "We've got to take every child's mind seriously," he says.

Logico-mathematical

The ability to think conceptually, to reason in an orderly manner, to investigate relationships in the physical world through experiment, and to explore more abstract relationships in the worlds of logic, computers, and mathematics.

Adult roles: Computer programmer, accountant, scientist, engineer, actuary, bank teller.

Signs of promise in the 5- or 6-year-old: Being able to notice numbers and patterns in his environment, as well as to estimate. The child may also invent strategies for counting and devise his own experiments.

---

5 **stay "on task"**   concentrate on completing an activity
6 **a behavior problem**   someone who causes problems
7 **gifted**   talented, with natural abilities
8 **catch on**   understand

Bodily-kinesthetic

A capacity to use the body, as Howard Gardner puts it, "in highly differentiated and skilled ways, for expressive as well as goal-oriented purposes." Both the fine motor movements of a craftsperson and the large-muscle movements of an athlete may be called upon.

Adult roles: Dancer, mime, athlete, actor, clown, comedian, and, in combination with spatial intelligence, craftsperson.

Signs of promise in the 5- or 6-year-old: Showing coordination, and ability in various sports or in dance.

A number of schools, inspired by Gardner's concept of multiple intelligences, are finding new ways of teaching that will not leave Sam, Amy—or, perhaps, your child—behind but will foster each child's potential. One of these schools is the Briarcliff School, in Shoreham, New York, where Marge Misiano teaches a combined kindergarten and first-grade class. Recently one morning I visited her classroom, where she and art teacher Ruth Kisch were teamteaching a project about how houses are built.

The class was divided into two groups. One was gathered around Misiano and discussing a collection of materials that had been brought in by a local builder: two-by-fours,[9] plasterboard, nails of different sizes, insulation, vinyl siding, shingles. The group discussion centered on which materials go inside a house and which go outside, which ones you will see when the house is completed and which you will not—all rather sophisticated subjects for a group this age.

The other group was clustered in a corner of the room with Kisch, who was showing them a photograph and a drawing of a house and asking them to identify the same features in both the photo and the drawing: doors, windows, shutters, a porch. Kisch then explained to them an architectural floor plan

---

Spatial

Good visual memory; the ability to recognize a shape when it appears in a new context, and to modify a visual image mentally. People with this intelligence can easily orient themselves in a house or outdoors and are good at reading maps.

Adult roles: Architect, graphic or industrial designer,

inventor, painter, picture framer, lighting specialist, and sculptor.

Signs of promise in the 5- or 6-year-old: Being drawn to all kinds of media—blocks, paints, clay, collage; enjoying taking things apart and putting them together; being able to learn from her mistakes.

---

9 **two-by-fours**   pieces of wood cut four inches wide and two inches thick

Intrapersonal	
The ability to recognize and discriminate among one's own feelings. We express our intrapersonal awareness in our gestures, facial expressions, and words. Adult roles: Poet, artist. Although many people with strong intrapersonal intelligence prefer to work alone, some may use their understanding of themselves to work with others as a therapist or counselor.	Signs of promise in the 5- or 6-year-old: Being able to talk insightfully about her own experience (for instance, saying to a parent something such as "Painting is fun, but it's hard for me" or "I knew I was going to cry, so I came and sat on your lap"); being aware of what she loves and fears.

of the house. A few minutes later, they turned to another floor plan, which she had drawn on a sheet of white paper laid out on the carpet. Kisch asked the children to build a block building by following the floor plan—a challenging task. When it was complete, the children sat down to draw it, making their version of the architectural drawing that they had studied at the beginning of the class.

How the theory of multiple intelligences works in the classroom.

The project, which was scheduled to continue for many weeks, had been carefully planned to tap[10] a range of the intelligences outlined by Howard Gardner in his book *Frames of Mind* (Basic Books). To understand the significance of approaching teaching and learning from an MI perspective,[11]

imagine what it would be like if Marge Misiano's class were to learn about building houses solely from a book or workbook. In such a case, the children's learning would be primarily linguistic. They would have little chance to work together or express their feelings about their own lives. They would be memorizing the phrase "two-by-four" without hefting[12] the real thing, looking at pictures of structures without the deeper and different knowledge that comes from trying to build or draw them.

As a consequence, some children's greatest abilities—one child's talent for leadership, another's skill as a builder—would never be encouraged, or even discovered. And some children—the Amys and Sams of the group—would not succeed.

Such children are described by Nancy Sims, another first-grade teacher at Briarcliff: "There were always those children who had so

---

10 **tap**   use, make use of
11 **perspective**   point of view
12 **hefting**   picking up or lifting something heavy

Linguistic

The ability to use language to express spoken and written meanings, to read and write. The linguistically gifted appreciate subtleties of meaning and grammar and often enjoy the sounds and rhythms of language.

Adult roles: Language skills can be used in many roles, including poet, politician, teacher, editor, journalist, salesperson, and actor.

Signs of promise in the 5- or 6-year-old: Being able to word-play; enjoy puns and rhyming; tell a detailed, fairly coherent story; enjoy reading.

---

much to offer but for whom school wasn't giving them the opportunity to show me what they could do."

A concern with the lost potential[13] of those who don't match the traditional profile of "school-smart"[14] has been the chief reason for educators' interest in Gardner's MI theory since he published *Frames of Mind* ten years ago. "We had one little boy," Briarcliff's principal, Margaret Daugherty, recalls, "who would have tested learning-disabled according to a standardized approach. He was slow in mastering literacy and slower at working in a large classroom setting. But actually he was a very deep thinker, he had a profound enjoyment of music, and he had spatial intelligence."

Influenced by Gardner's work, the Briarcliff Child Study Team ended up looking at this child differently from how they might have in the past. "We had to ask ourselves how we were going to look at him: as a child who has a problem, or as someone we should respond to differently?" Daugherty says. "He still received services, but we came to appreciate his strengths."

For many parents, particularly those whose children are having difficulty with the beginnings of reading and writing, MI theory offers another lens[15] through which their children can be seen. "If you think of intelligence in a narrow and static way as a matter of IQ scores," Daugherty notes, "then the curriculum will reflect that, and it is our belief that this limits the possibilities for students. It limits their development, which influences what happens when they become adults."

Phyllis La Farge, a contributing editor of Parents *magazine and a freelance writer, wishes that she had more kinesthetic intelligence.*

---

13 **potential**   possibilities, whatever might be accomplished
14 **"school-smart"**   recognized ways of showing intelligence at school
15 **lens**   way of seeing

4. **On your own.** Choose five unfamiliar words or phrases from the article and add them to the chart below. First guess the meaning of each word, using context. Then look up the words in your dictionary to check your guesses.

READING STRATEGY:
014 Using Context
See page 140.

Word	Word in context	My guess using context	Dictionary definition
toddler	"Ever since she was a toddler, 5-year-old Amy…	baby	a small child

Get together with several classmates. Tell what you found out about these words.

5. **Group Work.** Work together to answer the questions below. Then report your answers to the class.

CRITICAL THINKING STRATEGY:
016 Analyzing
See page 144.

a. Identify three important things you learned in this article.

b. Who do you think this article was written for? Why do you think this?

c. What do you think the writer's purpose is?

d. This article was actually written for the readers of *Parents* magazine. What about the article might be different if it had been written for a psychology journal?

e. Find something in the article that relates to your own experience and explain it to the people in your group.

6. **On your own.** In the article on pages 40–44, the writer Phyllis La Farge incorporates the ideas of other people into her writing. Look back over the article and underline each example of this. Then compare ideas with your classmates.

7. **Group Work.** Each of the people in the chart below is quoted directly in the article on pages 40–44. Refer to the article to complete the chart. Then answer the questions that follow.

WRITING STRATEGY:
008 Using Quotations
See page 129.

Person's Name	Credentials	Why quoted
Howard Gardner	professor of education author	has developed a theory of intelligence; is a well-known authority on the topic
Nancy Sims	_____	_____
Margaret Daugherty	_____	_____

a. Why do you think the writer of the article quoted these people?

b. Would the article be better, worse, or of the same quality if the quotations were deleted? Why?

WRITING STRATEGY:
001 Citing Sources
See page 115.

8. **On your own.** How would you punctuate the direct quotations in the sentences below?

• Writing about dramatic work, Cecily O'Neill and Alan Lambert (1982) warn Left to themselves, pupils are likely to work only at a superficial level in which they repeat or re-enact their existing insights.

• Judith Reiff (1922) argues that "Understanding theories of style can help teachers become better planners to meet the learning needs of their students."

• Gardner points out that our culture values some human abilities at the expense of others and that, as a result, we often fail to develop our children's potential. We've got to take every child's mind seriously he says.

• Influenced by Gardner's work, the Briarcliff Child Study Team ended up looking at one little boy differently from how they might have in the past. We had to ask ourselves how we were going to look at him: as a child who has a problem, or as someone we should respond to differently? Daugherty says. He still received services, but we came to appreciate his strengths, she adds.

9. **Pair Work.** In this excerpt from the article on pages 40–44, the writer Phyllis La Farge paraphrases another person's ideas. Read the paraphrase and then answer the questions below.

> Gardner believes that we have multiple intelligences (MIs)—although we are probably not equally well endowed in all of them—and that these intelligences are not restricted to the two cognitive areas of words and numbers, the ones most likely to be recognized and rewarded when children start school.

WRITING STRATEGY:
004 Paraphrasing
See page 121.

a. How is a paraphrase different from a direct quote?

b. When is it better to use a direct quote? When is it better to paraphrase?

c. Where else in the article on pages 40–44 does Phyllis La Farge paraphrase another person's ideas?

10. **On your own.** In the article on pages 40–44, La Farge both reports and interprets information. Read the example below, and then find another paragraph in the article in which she both reports and interprets information.

Example (excerpted from paragraph #8):

The group discussion centered on which materials go inside a house and which go outside, which ones you will see when the house is completed and which you will not— } reports

all rather sophisticated subjects for a group of this age. } interprets

Share ideas with your classmates.

11. **Writing Assignment.** Choose one of the intelligences identified in the article on pages 40–44. In one to two pages, explain this intelligence to a reader who is unfamiliar with Howard Gardner and his theory of multiple intelligences. In addition to expressing your own ideas, be sure to incorporate the ideas of others into your writing. Here are some steps you can follow:

a. Collect information about the intelligence you chose.

  • Look back over the article on pages 40–44 and take notes on the relevant information. Underline any information you may want to quote or paraphrase in your writing. Remember that you will need to introduce your reader to the theory of multiple intelligences.

  • Quickwrite about your experience with this type of intelligence.

  • Talk to different classmates and take notes. Find out about their experience with this intelligence. (Ask, for example: *What role does this intelligence play in your life? Do you think you have this intelligence? Was this intelligence rewarded in your school?*)

b. From these different sources, what do you know now about this intelligence? Look over your notes and think about what you want to say to your readers. In addition to describing the intelligence you chose, what points do you want to make?

c. Think about how you might organize your ideas and make some rough outlines. What do you want to say at the beginning of your essay? How will you get your reader's attention? What information and ideas do you want to include in the middle of your essay? How will you end your essay?

d. Write a first draft of your essay. Remember to include others' ideas to support the points you are making.

e. Exchange papers with a classmate and use the chart on page 154 to evaluate your classmate's essay.

f. Read your classmate's evaluation of your essay and then write one or more revised drafts of your essay. Then place your writing in your writing folder.

CRITICAL THINKING
STRATEGY:
022 Synthesizing
See page 156.

WRITING STRATEGY:
004 Paraphrasing
See page 121.

001 Citing Sources
See page 115.

WRITING STRATEGY:
006 Revising
See page 124.

Grammar Workshop 4a: adverb clauses

1. **Read the examples in the box and then answer the questions that follow.**

> *Examples*
>
> • **When you think of people whom you would describe as intelligent,** who comes to mind?
>
> • Who comes to mind **when you think of people whom you would describe as intelligent?**
>
> • **When the building was complete,** the children sat down to draw it.
>
> • **Ever since she was a toddler,** 5-year-old Amy has had excellent powers of concentration.
>
> • **Although Sam was having trouble learning to read,** his parents knew he was gifted.

   a. The **boldfaced** words in each sentence form an adverb clause. When do you use a comma with an adverb clause? When don't you?

   b. What words can you use to begin an adverb clause?

   c. What do you think determines the location of the adverb clause? *(Answers on page159.)*

2. **Underline the adverb clauses in these sentences.**

   a. Because our culture values some human abilities over others, we often fail to develop our children's potential.

   b. Since she read Gardner's book, her teaching has changed.

   c. Children's learning would be primarily linguistic if they learned about building houses only from books.

   d. The children would only be memorizing words like "two-by-four" unless their teacher gave them the chance to hold the real thing.

3. **Complete each sentence below.**

   a. Who do you talk to when _____?

   b. I'm studying English because_____ .

   c. When _____ , I sometimes go to the movies.

   d. Ever since I was a child, _____ .

   e. _____ although I find it hard to do.

49

Grammar Workshop 4b: reduced adverb clauses

1. **Read the sentences in the box and then answer the questions that follow.**

- Because they were inspired by Gardner's theory, a number of schools are finding new ways of teaching.
  Inspired by Gardner's theory, a number of schools are finding new ways of teaching.

- When the children had finished the building, they sat down to draw it.
  Having finished the building, the children sat down to draw it.

- We often fail to develop our children's potential because we value some abilities more than others.
  Valuing some abilities more than others, we often fail to develop our children's potential.

- While the children were working, the teacher moved around the classroom to talk to them.

---

   a. The first sentence in each pair has an adverb clause. The second sentence has a reduced adverb clause. What is the verb in each of these adverb clauses?

   b. The adverb clause in the last sentence cannot be reduced. Why? *(Answers on page159.)*

2. **Which sentence in each pair below has a reduced adverb clause? Check (✔) it.**

   a. ❏ Using Gardner's theory of multiple intelligences has helped the Briarcliff School to value different kinds of intelligence.

     ❏ Using Gardner's theory of multiple intelligences, the Briarcliff School has learned to value different kinds of intelligence.

   b. ❏ One group of children was gathered around Misiano, discussing a collection of building materials.

     ❏ Gathered around Misiano, one group of children was discussing a collection of building materials.

3. **Rewrite these sentences, using a complete adverb clause.**

   a. Having divided the class into groups, the teacher handed out the materials.

_____

   b. Having excellent powers of concentration, Amy can spend hours drawing.

_____

Using Writing to Understand a Text

In many college courses you will be required to read extensively. In this workshop, you will experiment with ways to use writing to understand a text. You will also try different strategies that can help you to manage long reading assignments.

1. **On your own.** Look quickly over the excerpt from a science textbook on pages 55–65. Which of the previewing strategies below would help you get ready to read the textbook excerpt? Check (✔) them.

READING STRATEGY:
010 Previewing
See page 136.

Previewing Strategies

❏ a. Look over the whole article to get an idea of its contents.

❏ b. Think about what you already know about the topic.

❏ c. Look at the visuals (pictures, graphs, tables, etc.) and read the captions.

❏ d. Ask yourself questions about the visuals and captions.

❏ e. Read the headings and subheadings and turn them into questions.

❏ f. Quickwrite for several minutes about the topic of the reading.

❏ g. Think about the role of the subject matter in your life.

❏ h. List things you already know about the topic. Then list things you would like to find out about the topic.

Example

Know	Want to Find Out
• Coffee has a lot of caffeine in it.	• What exactly is caffeine?
• It's not good to drink a lot of coffee.	• What happens to coffee beans after they are picked?
• There are many different kinds of coffee.	

Get together with several classmates and compare ideas.

2. **Group Work.** Working together on the textbook excerpt, try each of the previewing strategies in Activity 1 above. Then answer the questions below.

   a. Which strategies seem the most useful to you? Why?

   b. Which seem the least useful? Why?

   Share ideas with your classmates.

CRITICAL THINKING STRATEGY:
016 Analyzing
See page 144.

3. **On your own.** The chart below gives information about Table 14-1 on page 56 of the textbook excerpt. Choose a different table or figure from the same textbook excerpt, and use the questions below to make your own chart on separate paper.

Example (Table 14-1)

a. What seems to be the **purpose** of this visual?	• compares active compounds in five beverages
b. What **important words** come up in the visual?	• compounds, caffeine, theobromine, polyphenols
c. What **questions** does this visual raise for you?	• What is theobromine? • Why does tea have polyphenols but coffee doesn't?

Get together with a partner and share answers to the questions below.

a. What did you learn about the visual you studied? Tell your partner.

b. Do you think studying the visuals can help prepare you to read? If so, how?

c. Can the visuals help you learn new vocabulary? If so, how?

4. **Pair Work.** With your partner, quickly read through pages 55–58, looking for the writer's "promise" or statements of what is to come in the rest of the chapter. Underline the promise you find. Then answer the questions below.

a. Why do you think the writer included this "promise"?

b. What's the purpose of the information that comes before the writer's "promise"?

> **READING STRATEGY:**
> *009 Identifying the Writer's Thesis*
> See page 133.

5. **Pair Work.** You can often use context (the surrounding words and ideas) to get information about an unfamiliar word in a text. Often this useful information comes *after* the unfamiliar word. Follow the steps below to collect information about "caffeine."

a. Read the paragraph below and add what you learned about "caffeine" to the list of notes on page 54.

> **READING STRATEGY:**
> *014 Using Context*
> See page 140.

Coffee, tea, and cocoa are stimulants because they contain the alkaloid caffeine and its relatives, which cause particular physiological reactions in humans. As was pointed out in Chapter 13, caffeine is a central nervous system stimulant and a mild diuretic. The caffeine in a cup of coffee reaches the bloodstream 5 minutes after the liquid is swallowed. As it circulates throughout the body, it stimulates the heart, increases stomach acidity and urine output, and causes a 10 percent rise in the metabolic rate.

Notes on caffeine

- it's an alkaloid

- causes physiological reactions in people

- _____

- _____

- _____

- _____

b. Look over your notes about caffeine. Try to find a useful way to reorganize the information about caffeine. Experiment by adding information to the chart below.

CAFFEINE

Characteristics	Effects of
an alkaloid	causes physiological reactions
_____	_____
_____	_____
_____	_____

Compare charts with your classmates.

READING STRATEGY:
015 Writing Margin Notes
See page 143.

6. **On your own.** Reread pages 55–58 of the textbook chapter. In the margin next to each paragraph, answer these questions.

   a. What is the paragraph about?

   b. What questions do you have about the information in this paragraph?

7. **On your own.** Read pages 58–63. As you read, underline the ideas that seem the most important to you. Then answer the questions below.

   a. Do you think it is useful to underline information in a textbook?

   b. Do you think it is possible to underline too many things? If so, why?

   c. Why might it be difficult to underline the most important information on the first reading?

   Share answers with your classmates.

8. **On your own.** Read the rest of the textbook chapter. Experiment with underlining and writing margin notes.

⬛◆⬛◆⬛◆⬛◆⬛◆⬛◆

READING STRATEGY:
013 Underlining
See page 139.

Stimulating Beverages

The drinking of coffee, tea, and chocolate milk has become such an integral part of American life that people take it for granted. Many Americans profess that they could not face the morning without a cup of coffee, and a coffee break or tea time is enjoyed by most people in the western world who need a lift at the end of the day. People drink these beverages not only for the boost they provide but for their flavor as well. Other stimulating beverages, such as mate, kola, and guaraná, have become locally important for the same reasons, but coffee, tea, and cocoa reign supreme on a worldwide basis (Fig. 14-1).

All these beverages are stimulants because they contain the alkaloid caffeine and its relatives (Table 14-1 and Fig. 14-2), which cause particular physiolog-

Figure 14-1: This drawing represents the world's three most important nonalcoholic beverages and the civilizations associated with them: coffee in an Arab's cup, tea being drunk by a Chinese, and cocoa in an American Indian's goblet. (From Dufour, Philippe, Traitez nouveaux et curieux du café, du thé, et du chocolat, Lyons, 1671.)

TABLE 14-1 ACTIVE COMPOUNDS IN THE WORLD'S MAJOR STIMULATING BEVERAGES*

Plant Part	Caffeine	Theobromine	Polyphenols
Coffee, unroasted, dried	1–1.5	—	—
Teas, dried leaves	2.5–4.5	—	25.0
Cacao			
Dried nibs	0.6	1.7	3.6
Fresh cotyledons	0.8	2.4	5.2
Kola, fresh seeds	2.0	—	—
Guaraná, dried fruit	3.0–4.5	—	—

*Figures given in percent weight. Amounts of the compounds in a particular beverage depend on how the beverage is made.

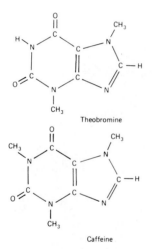

Figure 14-2: Caffeine and theobromine both have stimulating effects.

ical reactions in humans. Caffeine is a central nervous system stimulant and a mild diuretic. The caffeine in a cup of coffee reaches the bloodstream 5 minutes after the liquid is swallowed. As it circulates throughout the body, it stimulates the heart, increases stomach acidity and urine output, and causes a 10 percent rise in the metabolic rate. If a person is tired, caffeine makes that person more alert, because it mimics the feelings produced when the body releases the hormone adrenaline. In excessive doses, however, caffeine can produce unpleasant symptoms. One gram of the compound (about 10 cups of coffee) causes anxiety, headache, dizziness, insomnia, heart palpitations, and even mild delirium. Heavy drinkers of tea or coffee can develop a tolerance to caffeine and can even suffer withdrawal symptoms, such as headaches, when they quit the habit. Caffeine ranks today as the most widely used psychoactive drug in the world, not only because of the large number of coffee and tea drinkers, but also because it is added to numerous soft drinks and various medications (Table 14-2). Unfortunately, children who have neither the body mass nor the tolerance for large amounts of caffeine consume appreciable quantities of soft drinks. There is some debate about the permanent effects of moderate caffeine intake on adults, but doctors now advise pregnant women to reduce or eliminate caffeine consumption because studies have shown that babies born to mothers who consume caffeinated beverages have a 4 percent lower birthweight than do those born to mothers who did not drink such beverages.

TABLE 14-2 AMOUNTS OF CAFFEINE IN COMMONLY CONSUMED BEVERAGES AND MEDICINES

Item	Caffeine, mg
Coffee	
5-oz cup, drip method	146
5-oz cup, percolator method	110
5-oz cup, instant	53
5-oz cup, decaffeinated	2
Tea	
5-oz cup, brewed 1 min	9–33
5-oz cup, brewed 3-5 min	20–50
12 oz, canned	22–36
Cocoa and chocolate	
6 oz, made with canned powder	10
1 oz milk chocolate	6
1 oz (1 square) baking chocolate	35
Soft drinks	
12 oz Mountain Dew	52
12 oz Dr. Pepper (reg./sugar free)	37–38
12 oz Pepsi, regular	37
12 oz Coca Cola	34
Nonprescription drugs	
Stimulants	
NoDoz (standard dose)	200
Pain relievers (standard dose)	
Excedrin	132
Midol	65
Anacin	64
Cold remedies	
Dristan	32
Diuretics (standard dose)	
Aqua-Ban	200
Weight-control aids (daily dose)	
Prolamine	280
Dietac	200

Source: Adapted from *Consumer Reports*, Vol. 46, 1981, pp. 598, 599. Not all soft drinks and medications containing caffeine are included. Consumers should read the labels of such products to determine whether they contain caffeine. Several manufacturers have recently removed the caffeine from the form of their products labeled "caffeine-free."

The way in which caffeine and related compounds work is something of a mystery, but biochemical studies have suggested that these compounds block adenosine, a chemical messenger that occurs naturally in the body. When adenosine attaches to special receptors on the surfaces of brain cells, it dilates arteries, suppresses locomotor activity, and produces sedation. Caffeine, theophylline, and theobromine block the attachment of adenosine to the surfaces of these cells and thus maintain or cause a feeling of alertness and activity. These compounds, especially theophylline, also relax the smooth muscles of the bronchial system. As a result, theophylline is used to treat asthma.

In view of their worldwide social and economic importance, we discuss coffee, tea, and cacao in detail, looking at the places where humans first used them for beverages, their discovery by Europeans, their methods of cultivation, and the processing necessary before each reaches a cup or a glass. Because of their limited use, mate, kola, and guaraná are discussed only briefly.

Coffee

In terms of its economic value, coffee is one of the world's most important commodities traded annually on the international market. Although the genus *Coffea* (Rubiaceae) is native to eastern Africa, comparatively few Africans drink coffee. The earliest records of coffee use come from Ethiopia, where natives chewed leaves and fruits gathered from wild trees growing in the forests. A mixture of ground-roasted, or green coffee fruits, and fat was taken along on hunts as a survival staple similar to the pemmican (a mixture of dried buffalo meat and fat) used by American Indians. Caffeine that dispelled fatigue and relieved hunger was leached out of the leaves or fruit during chewing. Beverage making seems to have been a later development, and some authors have suggested that an alcoholic beverage was made from the fruit before a nonalcoholic one was produced.

Coffee probably arrived in Yemen some time before the fourteenth century. As alluded by the name *Coffea arabica,* the Arabs were the first to brew coffee (Fig. 14-3). Coffee drinking spread from Arabia to Egypt by 1510 and to Italy by 1616. Alarmed at the rapidly spreading popularity of coffee drinking, the priests of

TABLE 14-3 PLANTS DISCUSSED IN THIS CHAPTER

Common Name	Scientific Name	Family	Native to
Achiote	*Bixa orellana*	Bixaceae	Mexico
Cacao	*Theobroma cacao*	Sterculiaceae	Mexico
Chicory	*Cichorium intybus*	Asteraceae	Europe
Coffee			Africa
Arabian	*Coffea arabica*	Rubiaceae	
Liberian	*Coffea liberica*		
Robusta	*Coffea canephora*		
Guaraná	*Paullinia cupana*	Sapindaceae	South America
Kola	*Cola nitida*	Sterculiaceae	West Africa
Mate	*Ilex paraguariensis*	Aquifoliaceae	South America
Tea	*Camellia sinensis*	Theaceae	China

Vienna urged the Pope to ban the drink, as it had come from the land of "infidels."   After trying the brew, however, Pope Clement VIII promptly baptized it, making it a Christian beverage. By 1650, coffee had arrived in England, where it became an important part of the social and political environment. England alone had over 3,000 coffee-houses by 1675, many of which functioned as forums for political and religious debates. The increasing attendance at those houses and the spread of the ideas discussed within them so alarmed King Charles II that he labeled them "seminaries of sedition" and tried to have them closed. The uproar that resulted from his edict forced Charles to rescind his order, and soon the demand for coffee sent all of Europe looking for new sources of the seeds.

For years the Arabs monopolized the coffee trade and prevented the cultivation of coffee by other countries.

Figure 14-3: A lithograph of an Arabian coffee service, redrawn from *A Thousand and One Arabian Nights.*

They cleverly dipped the seeds in boiling water before marketing to kill the embryos and prevent germination. Eventually, however, the Dutch managed to secure live seeds from Mocha, a city in Yemen on the Red Sea, the traditional Arabian source of coffee. With these viable seeds, the Dutch started extensive plantations in the East Indies, breaking the Arabian monopoly. Trees from these plantations were sent to the botanical garden in Amsterdam in 1706, but only one survived the journey. Seeds from this single tree were later given to other botanical gardens in Europe, including the Jardin des Plantes in Paris.

The tree in the conservatory of the Paris garden was considered a curiosity by most people, but one man realized its potential value. This young Frenchman, Gabriel de Clieu, argued that if coffee grew well for the Dutch in the East Indies, it should grow equally well for the French in the West Indies. Stories vary as to how de Clieu obtained seeds, but they all agree that in about 1723 he arrived in Martinique with a single surviving offspring of the Parisian tree. From this small island, seeds were dispersed throughout the Antilles and to French Guiana. De Clieu was not the first to introduce coffee to the new world. Records show that the Dutch had started plantings in Suriname in 1717. Eventually, growers in Brazil (Fig. 14-4), which now leads the world in coffee production (Table 14-4), obtained seeds from either Suriname or French Guiana. By 1729 Brazil was producing 200,000 bags of coffee annually.

Although *Coffea arabica* has figured most prominently in history and now accounts for more than 90 percent of the world's coffee

Figure 14-4: From its origins in Africa, virtually one clone of *Coffea arabica* spread around the world and established successful coffee production in the West Indies and South America. On the left is a drawing of Lieutenant de Clieu tending the coffee plant he brought from France to Martinique. (Adapted from N.W. Simmonds, 1976, *Evolution of Crop Plants*, New York: Longman.)

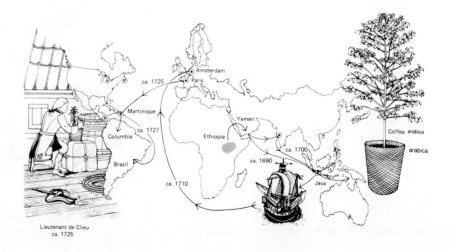

production, it is not the only species of the genus that yields coffee-producing seeds. *Coffea canephora,* known as robusta coffee, is the source of 9 percent of the world's coffee, and *Coffea liberica,* or Liberian coffee, contributes about 1 percent. The predominant use of *Coffea arabica* can be attributed to several of its characteristics. First, it is self-fertilizing and self-compatible. The successful introduction of coffee into the New World was possible because

TABLE 14-4 WORLD PRODUCTION OF COFFEE, TEA, AND COCOA

| Crop | Top Five Countries | | Top Five Continents | | |
	Country	1,000 m.t.	Continent	1,000 m.t.	Total m.t.
Coffee	Brazil	1,298	South America	2,654	5,919
	Colombia	1,050	Africa	1,216	
	Indonesia	421	North/Central America	1,049	
	Ivory Coast	240	Asia	953	
	Ethiopia	216 *	Oceania	48	
Tea	India	703 *	Asia	1,991	2,473
	China	580 *	Africa	300	
	Kenya	188 *	South America	64	
	Sri Lanka	179 *	Oceania	9	
	Indonesia	163	North/Central America	1	
Cocoa	Ivory Coast	700 *	Africa	1,259	2,329
	Brazil	343	South America	512	
	Ghana	280 *	Asia	408	
	Malaysia	217 *	North/Central America	108	
	Indonesia	175	Oceania	42	

*Indicates an estimated or unofficial figure.
Note: Only crops of major importance in international trade are included. Figures from the former U.S.S.R. are not added into those of Europe or Asia. The abbreviation m.t. = metric tons.
Source: Data from *FAO Production Yearbook for 1992,* vol. 46, 1993. Rome: FAO.

the plant sent to Amsterdam was able to produce viable seed by self-fertilization, whereas the other two beverage-yielding species are self-incompatible. More importantly, however, coffee made from *Coffea arabica* has a better flavor than that made from the other two species. Robusta coffee is grown primarily for use in blended coffees or to make decaffeinated or instant coffee, where the taste is disguised or altered. Liberian coffee, the most bitter of the three, is used primarily as a filler in mixtures with other coffees.

All cultivated species of *Coffea* are small trees with glossy leaves and fragrant, jasminelike white flowers produced in the leaf axils (Fig. 14-5). The fruits take 7 to 9 months to mature into what is called a cherry. Because it comes from an inferior ovary, the cherry

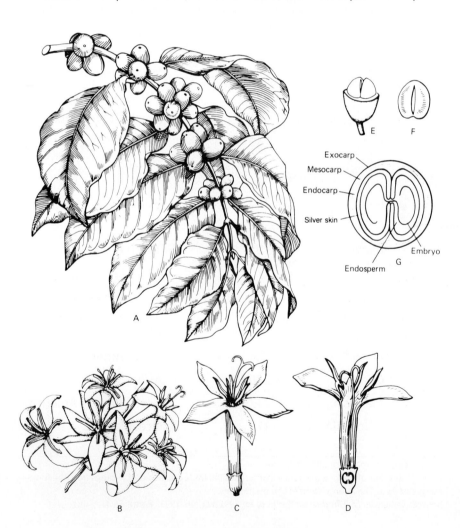

Figure 14-5: A) A branch of coffee with clusters of berries in the leaf axils, redrawn from Baillon. B) Cluster of jasminelike flowers. C) Individual flower. D) Cross-section of individual flower. E) Position of the two seeds in the fleshy fruit. F) Ventral (flattened) side of seed. G) Cross section of whole berry showing component parts.

is an accessory "berry" with a tough outer layer composed of the floral cup and exocarp, the fleshy mesocarp, and the thin, fibrous endocarp, or "parchment" (Fig. 14-5). Within the endocarp, two seeds press together in such a way that the inner side of each one is flattened. Each seed, commonly called a bean, is surrounded by a thin, silvery seed coat. The seed itself is composed mostly of endosperm surrounding a small, curved embryo.

Because coffee trees cannot tolerate sustained freezing, cultivation is restricted to tropical and subtropical latitudes. An average coffee plant produces its first crop after 3 years, and it has a productive life of about 40 years. Most coffee is grown today in open orchards, but some cultivators claim that superior coffee is produced by shaded trees. Arabian coffee is generally grown on hillsides at altitudes of 1,500 to 2,000 m (4,920 to 6,560 ft), but robusta and Liberian coffee are generally grown at low elevations. Because of the size of the tree and the slope of the terrain on which it is usually grown, Arabian coffee is seldom harvested mechanically. Moreover, berries ripen sequentially on branches of the trees, and so only a few can be picked from a branch at any time (Fig. 14-6).

Figure 14-6: A coffee picker such as this Colombian can pick 91 kg (200 lb) a day. About 2,000 beans (1,000 cherries) are needed to produce a pound (453 g) of roasted, ground coffee. (United Nations photo by Jerry Frank.)

Coffee Processing

To produce aromatic ground coffee, the seeds must be separated from the rest of the fruit and roasted. Either a wet or a dry process can be used to remove the outer fruit parts. In the dry process, the fresh fruits are dried in the sun and the pericarp is subsequently rasped away. In the wet process (Fig. 14-7), which produces a superior final flavor, the fresh fruits are depulped by a machine and the seeds are washed. The wet seeds are then allowed to ferment for 12 to 24 hours. This fermentation is not the same process involved in the production of alcohol. In the cases of coffee, cocoa, tea, and kola, fermentation refers to an enzymatic, chemical alteration of several compounds. Coffee fermentation produces substances that will eventually develop into the characteristic coffee aroma and taste. It also causes the seeds to take on a gray-green hue. After fermentation, the seeds are dried by being turned in the sun for at least 1 week. Any remaining endocarp and the seed coats are removed mechanically before shipping. Subsequent processing typically occurs in the country where the coffee is consumed.

Roasting is done in cylinders that simultaneously tumble and heat the seeds. During the roasting process, water-soluble aromas develop and begin to diffuse. Beans are roasted at temperatures of 200 to 230°C (392 to 446°F) for 10-15 minutes, depending on the size of the roaster and the degree of roasting. As the beans roast, sugars are caramelized, starches are hydrolyzed, and the cellular matrix breaks down, allowing the beans to swell as gases are released. The kind of roast depends on how long the beans are held in the roasters, and thus on the final temperature the beans are allowed to reach (200°C for light roast, 230°C for dark). The beans are quickly cooled with water or cold air to stop the process and slow the loss of aromatic oils.

Despite the statement that dark-roast coffees are "stronger" than light roasts, they are not stronger in the sense of containing more caffeine. Dark roasts just seem stronger because they have more flavor than do light roasts. Dark-roast beans are larger than light-roast beans because they swell more during roasting, and they feel oily because their higher roasting temperatures cause some of the aromatic oils to come to the surface. Light- or medium-roast beans are dry on the outside. Almost all the roasting for American palates is of either the light or medium type. Europeans and Latin Americans, by contrast, prefer dark roasts, one of which is commonly called espresso. It should be noted that espresso is a method of making coffee that involves forcing steam through the grounds. Espresso coffee can be made with light-roast coffee, but it is generally made with deeply roasted beans. Once roasting is complete, the beans can be shipped whole or ground and packaged (often under a vacuum to preserve the flavor) before being shipped to market.

Figure 14-7: Steps in the processing of coffee: A) selective hand picking of only the red, ripe berries; B) depulping and washing the berries; C) fermenting the seeds; D) drying the beans; E) transporting the green beans to market; and F) an older method of roasting the beans. (Modern roasters use automatic tumblers.)

◻◈◈◻◻◈◻◻◈◻◈◻◻

READING STRATEGY:
011 Quickwriting
See page 136.

9. **On your own.** Reread only pages 63–65 of the textbook chapter. Then close your book and quickwrite for two minutes about what you remember.

   Did quickwriting help you to understand and remember what you read? Share your answers with your classmates.

10. **Writing Assignment.** How can you use writing to learn academic course material? For this writing assignment, you will experiment with taking split-page study notes. Follow the instructions below to get started.

    a. Look back at the textbook excerpt on pages 55–65 and identify the terms, concepts, and processes that you think are important. On a separate paper, record these terms and concepts in the left column of a split-page chart like this:

SPLIT-PAGE CHART

Important terms, concepts & processes	Supporting information
caffeine	stimulates central nervous system
history of coffee use	

    b. In the right column of the chart, list important supporting information about each term or concept. Be brief and try to use your own words.

    c. Get together with several classmates and compare study notes. Which important terms, concepts, and processes did you all list? Are there any other terms and concepts that you want to add to your notes? Did you include too much supporting information, not enough, or just the right amount?

    d. Revise your study notes and place a copy of them in your writing folder.

◻◈◈◻◻◈◻◻◈◻◈◻◻

WRITING STRATEGY:
006 Revising
See page 124.

Grammar Workshop 5a: word forms

1. Read the examples in the box and then answer the questions that follow.

> *Examples*
>
> - Caffeine is a central nervous system **stimulant.**
>   Caffeine **stimulates** the central nervous system.
>
> - Doctors now advise pregnant women to reduce or eliminate their caffeine **consumption.**
>   Doctors now say that pregnant women shouldn't **consume** caffeine.
>
> - **Consuming** less coffee is doctors' advice for pregnant women.
>   Doctors' advice for pregnant women is **to consume** little to no coffee.

   a. How are the **boldfaced** words in each group different?

   b. In your writing, why might it be useful to know the different forms of a word? *(Answers on pages 159–160.)*

2. Paraphrase the sentences below. Try to use the words in parentheses.

   a. There is some debate about the permanent effects of moderate caffeine intake on adults. (affects)

   _____

   _____

   b. Alarmed at the rapidly spreading popularity of coffee drinking, the priests of Vienna urged the Pope to ban the drink. (popular)

   _____

   _____

   c. For years the Arabs monopolized the coffee trade. (had a monopoly of)

   _____

   _____

d. Only one man realized the potential value of the coffee tree in the Jardin des Plantes in Paris. (valuable)

_____

_____

e. *Coffea arabica* accounts for more than 90 percent of the world's coffee production. (produced)

_____

_____

3. Choose a word from the chart to complete each sentence below.

Noun	Verb	Adjective
stimulant	stimulate	stimulating
popularity	popularize	popular
value	value	valuable
advice	advise	advisable

a. Mate, kola, coffee, tea, cocoa, and guaraná are _____ beverages. In other words, they _____ the body's central nervous system.

b. Of these beverages, coffee, tea, and cocoa are the most _____ world wide, with large numbers of drinkers across the globe.

c. Doctors now _____ pregnant women to reduce or eliminate caffeine consumption.

d. Traded annually on the international market, coffee is a _____ economic commodity.

Grammar Workshop 5b: rearranging information

1. **Read the sentences in the box and then answer the questions that follow.**

   > • Caffeine, an alkaloid, stimulates the central nervous system. _____
   >
   > • The alkaloid caffeine stimulates the central nervous system. _____
   >
   > • One central nervous system stimulant is the alkaloid caffeine. _____
   >
   > • One stimulant of the central nervous system is the alkaloid caffeine. _____
   >
   > • One thing that stimulates the central nervous system is the alkaloid caffeine. _____

   a. The sentences in the box communicate similar information. However, by rearranging the information, we changed the focus of the sentence. Underline the focus of each sentence.

   b. In a paragraph, which of the two sentences below could follow each statement in the box? Write 1 or 2 at the end of each sentence above.

      1. Another is theobromine.

      2. It also increases stomach acidity and urine output as it circulates through the body.
      (Answers on page 160.)

2. **Think of different ways to arrange the information in each sentence below.**

   a. The caffeine in a cup of coffee reaches the bloodstream in five minutes.

      In five minutes, _____ .

   b. Theophylline is a compound that relaxes the smooth muscles of the bronchial system.

      The compound theophylline _____ .

      One compound that _____ .

   c. Adrenaline is a hormone that makes a person feel more alert.

      The hormone _____

      _____ .

d. The way in which caffeine and related compounds work is something of a mystery.

It's something of a mystery _____

_____ .

How caffeine and related compounds work _____

_____ .

Caffeine and related compounds work in a way _____

_____ .

e. When adenosine attaches to special receptors on the surfaces of brain cells, it produces sedation.

Adenosine produces sedation when _____

_____ .

Attaching to special receptors _____

_____ .

Sedation is produced _____

_____ .

Grammar Workshop 5c: sentence beginnings

1. **Read the paragraph in the box and then answer the questions that follow.**

> **The way in which caffeine and related compounds work** is something of a mystery, but biochemical studies have suggested that these compounds block adenosine, a chemical messenger that occurs naturally in the body. **Caffeine, theophylline, and theobromine** block the attachment of adenosine to the surfaces of these cells and thus maintain or cause a feeling of alertness and activity. **These compounds**, especially theophylline, also relax the smooth muscles of the bronchial system. **As a result,** theophylline is used to treat asthma.

    a. There are lots of different ways to begin a sentence. Why do you think the writer of this paragraph chose to begin each sentence in this way?

    b. How does the beginning of a sentence help the reader follow the writer's thinking? *(Answers on page 160.)*

2. **Which sentence best completes the paragraph? Check (✔) it.**

> The way I study for an essay exam is to first be sure I have read and understood all the required material. I must know all about the subject, both inside-out and outside-in. One thing I do to study is to rewrite my notes on any key concepts that might end up on the test.
>
> _____

    ❏ I want to get into the habit of writing about things the test could cover.

    ❏ By doing this I am getting into the habit of writing about things the test could cover.

    ❏ I get into the habit of writing about things the test could cover by doing this.

3. Which sentence best completes the paragraph? Check (✔) it.

> When I'm handed an essay test, the first thing I do is to read the questions several times to myself. _____
>
> _____
>
> If the question asks me to define something, I need to be sure I am defining it and not simply describing it. If I am asked to contrast two things, I had better not compare them. Writing down a few notes does not equal writing an essay. Not only is it important to define, describe, or compare—whatever the question asks me to do—but I have to show that I can follow directions.

❏ The most important aspect of taking an essay exam is understanding exactly what a question is asking me to do.

❏ When I take an exam, it's important to understand exactly what a question is asking me to do.

❏ Understanding exactly what a question is asking me to do is the most important aspect of taking an essay exam.

Responding to Exam Questions

On examinations in your academic courses, you will have to show your knowledge of course material. In most cases, your instructor will evaluate your responses based on how clearly, accurately, and comprehensively you answer the questions. In this workshop, you will look at different kinds of exam questions, evaluate several exam responses, and then practice writing your own answers to typical exam questions.

1. **On your own.** Put a checkmark next to the kinds of tests you have taken.

   ❏ A true-false test. (You decide whether statements are true or false.)

   ❏ A multiple-choice test. (Questions are followed by several answers. You must choose the correct one.)

❑ A fill-in-the-blank test. (Statements are incomplete. Sometimes you choose from a list of possible answers to complete the statements.)

❑ A short-answer exam. (Questions require you to write a short answer of several sentences.)

❑ An essay exam. (Questions require you to write a page or two in response.)

Tell your classmates which type of exam you like least and why. Discuss why you think some teachers give essay exams. Why might a teacher <u>not</u> give them?

CRITICAL THINKING STRATEGY:
016 Analyzing
See page 144.

2. **Pair Work.** Study the essay exam questions below. Circle the important instruction words. Underline the important content words. (You don't need to know the meaning of every word in the exam questions to complete this activity.)

a. (Discuss) how <u>microbial fermentation</u> is used in <u>food preservation</u>. Include (examples) and (explain) how the <u>process</u> works. *(from a biology exam)*

b. Describe the malting process. Include a discussion of the importance of the malting process to beer production. *(from a biology exam)*

c. According to Newton's 3rd law, each team in a tug-of-war pulls with equal force on the other team. What, then, determines which team wins? *(from a physics exam)*

d. What is a short circuit? Why will it cause a fuse or circuit breaker in your house to blow? *(from a physics exam)*

e. Explain one member of each pair below by contrasting it to the other. Give examples. *(from a linguistics exam)*

pidgin/creole   coherence/cohesion

f. Compare and contrast the life of Renaissance women with that of modern women. *(from a history exam)*

g. Identify the three major budget philosophies that prevail in American capitalistic thought and compare their approaches to government spending. *(from an economics exam)*

h. Compare the political careers of Santa Anna, Benito Juárez, and Porfirio Díaz. Which leader do you think had the greatest impact on Mexico? Explain. *(from a history exam)*

Compare ideas with another pair of your classmates.

3. **Group Work.** On pages 76–79 there are four essay questions from an economic botany exam. Following each question is a student's response. Use the ideas below to analyze and evaluate each exam question and answer. (Remember that you don't need to know the meaning of the technical terms to do this activity.)

a. Read the four *questions* aloud in your group. What are the important instruction words in each question? What are the important content words? Compare ideas with the other groups in your class.

b. Read the *answer* to each question on pages 76–79 and complete the chart that follows each answer. (Note that the second question in each chart is answered for you.) Then compare ideas with the other groups in your class.

> **CRITICAL THINKING STRATEGY:**
> *020 Evaluating*
> See page 153.

Question 1
Describe the production of paper. Consider historical aspects as well as production today. Be sure to discuss pulp production.

Robert's Answer

Paper has been around since the early Egyptians. They used the papyrus plant, peeling off the green to leave the parenchyma cells. In China, Tsi Lin, the first person to make paper, took the plique of the rice paper plant, beat it to get the pulp out of it, and spread it on a bamboo screen to flatten and dry. The French, however, were the first to produce the kind of paper we use today. They incorporated the pulp that was beaten out, and they used continuous screen rollers and dryers.

When the printing press was developed, there was an increase in the demand for paper. People started using old linen fibers as a source to make paper. After linen ran out, people began to raid tombs and remove the linen wrappings of the bodies. To avoid having to do this, others began to use wood as a source.

Wood yields two kinds of pulp, mechanical and chemical. Mechanical pulp contains cellulose fibers, with lignin throughout. Chemical pulp is mechanical pulp with the lignin leached out. Paper bags from supermarkets are made from mechanical pulp, their brown color resulting from the lignin in the pulp. Chemical pulp yields a better quality of white paper.

1.

1. Did the writer follow the instructions in the question?   YES   NO

2. Is the information in the answer correct?   (YES)   NO

3. How clear is the answer?   VERY   SOMEWHAT   NOT AT ALL

4. Is the answer complete?   YES   NO

Question 2

Discuss, with the aid of diagrams, the structure of wood. Be sure to discuss the appearance of tangentially and radially sawn ("quarter sawn") boards of the same species. For good measure, include a consideration of wood expansion and shrinkage with changes in humidity.

Robert's Answer

Wood is arranged to the inside with xylem cells, used to conduct water, and to the outside with phloem cells. A lateral layer of cells, called the vascular cambium, connects the xylem and phloem cells and is capable of dividing into more xylem to the inside and more phloem to the outside.

The annual rings reflect each year's growth—from the spring, when cells become large and divide, to the winter, when they stop dividing. From the rings, we can tell the approximate age of a tree.

There are three sections in which a log can be cut. When it is cut horizontally, we call it a cross-section. A radial section is when a log is cut vertically directly down the center, which yields quarter-sawn pieces of wood. A tangential section is cut vertically on either side of the center, or radial section.

The grain, which is the arrangement of ray parenchyma cells, is what determines the direction of expansion when water is absorbed into the wood. Wood expands along the direction of the grain. Porosity is the way the vessels are dispersed throughout the wood.

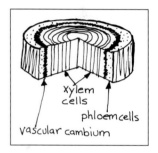

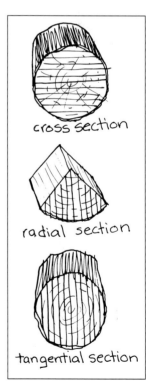

cross section

radial section

tangential section

2.

1. Did the writer follow the instructions in the question? YES   NO

2. Is the information in the answer correct? (YES)   NO

3. How clear is the answer? VERY   SOMEWHAT   NOT AT ALL

4. Is the answer complete? YES   NO

> **Question 3**
> Explain why many crops are more successful when they are cultivated in regions to which they are not native.

Nicole's Answer

Crops tend to be more successful in regions to which they are not native. The reason is that certain diseases have evolved and invaded these plants. An example of this is what happened to rye. In the 1950s, rye rust disease *(Clavicepts purepur fungus)* parasitized the rye plant. It invaded the sclerotiums of rye by producing spores, lysergic acid, and ergotamine. This disease had profound effects on humans. Lysergic acid produced hallucinations and ergotamine produced gangrene in individuals who consumed too much diseased rye. It was a problem in areas where bread was produced using rye. Now rye is grown in many areas.

3.

1. Did the writer follow the instructions in the question?   YES   NO

2. Is the information in the answer correct?   (YES)   NO

3. How clear is the answer?   VERY   SOMEWHAT   NOT AT ALL

4. Is the answer complete?   YES   NO

Question 4
Describe the processing of tea or chocolate, and explain how differences in the processing result in different forms of the product.

Nicole's Answer

Three different teas can be produced using three slightly different methods of processing. Producing green tea involves picking the leaves, bruising them in order to disrupt cell structure, drying them quickly, and then packaging them. The process is a bit different for black and oolong tea. While both first undergo the same picking and bruising stages as green tea, a fermentation process then comes into play. This autolytic process destroys the embryo. Then the leaves are dried by sunlight or artificial light. The difference between the two is that black tea is fermented longer than oolong.

4.

1. Did the writer follow the instructions in the question?   YES   NO

2. Is the information in the answer correct?   (YES)   NO

3. How clear is the answer?   VERY   SOMEWHAT   NOT AT ALL

4. Is the answer complete?   YES   NO

◻◇◪◻◻◇◪◻◻◇◪◻◻◇
┌─────────────────────┐
│ CRITICAL THINKING   │
│ STRATEGY: │
│ *022 Synthesizing* │
│ See page 156.   │
└─────────────────────┘

4. **Pair Work.** Below are the grades that Robert and Nicole received on their answers to the exam questions in Activity 3. With a partner, tell why you think they received these grades (12 points is the highest possible grade).

Robert's answer to question 1:	10 points
Robert's answer to question 2:	12 points
Nicole's answer to question 3:	10 points
Nicole's answer to question 4:	12 points

Share ideas with another pair. With the class, then brainstorm ways to improve the answers with the lower marks.

5. **Group Work.** Look back at the textbook chapter on pages 55–65. What essay exam questions might a teacher ask? Work together to come up with four questions, using instruction words from the list below.

Commonly-Used Instruction Words

- Discuss how…is used…
- Explain how…works.

- Describe _____ process.
- Explain the importance of…
- Explain…by contrasting it with…

- Trace the development of…
- Define…and explain its importance.
- Compare…
- Evaluate…

---

a. _____

_____

b. _____

_____

c. _____

_____

d. _____

_____

Share your questions with the other groups in your class.

6. **Group Work.** Divide the questions below among the groups in your class. Working in your group, use your study notes from Activity 10 on page 66 to answer your group's questions. If necessary look back at the textbook excerpt, pages 55–65, to find additional information. Then decide what information you would include in each answer.

   a. About 5 minutes after you drink a cup of coffee, you feel a physiological reaction. Explain the reaction.

   b. Define *adenosine* and explain its role in the body's reaction to stimulants.

   c. Briefly discuss the Arabian monopoly of the coffee trade and how it was broken.

   d. Classify *Coffea* into three species and explain the differences.

   e. Briefly describe the processing of coffee from tree to market.

   f. Briefly discuss the political and social effects of coffee's arrival in England in the 1600s.

   g. Contrast the production of dark roast coffee to that of light roast beans.

   h. Analyze the world production of coffee by continent.

   i. Explain why *Coffea arabica* dominates the market.

Report to the class on your group's discussion.

▣◈▣◧◇▣◻◻◈▣◻◧◻◈◻

WRITING STRATEGY:
*003 Organizing
Ideas*
See page 119.

7. Group Work. "Organizer" sentences help readers stay on track by announcing what body of information comes next. Study the organizers below and tell what information the writer is likely to present next. The first one is done for you.

a. The predominant use of *Coffea arabica* can be attributed to several of its characteristics.

> What will come next?   *The writer will identify the characteristics of C. arabica that explain its dominance of the market.*

b. Today, two basic processes are used to remove caffeine from coffee beans.

> What will come next?   _____

> _____

c. The processing of tea leaves depends on the final kind of tea desired.

> What will come next?   _____

> _____

d. Instant tea dates from 1885, when an Englishman, John Brown, developed a dry paste made from tea extract, evaporated milk, and sugar.

> What will come next?   _____

> _____

e. Cacao was first encountered by Europeans when Columbus landed in Nicaragua.

> What will come next?   _____

> _____

8. Writing Assignment. Choose one essay question from the list in Activity 6. Then follow the instructions below to answer it. Your teacher will decide if you will do this writing assignment as homework or as a timed writing exam in class. If it is a practice exam, your teacher will decide if you can bring notes.

a. Make a plan. Decide how much time you would spend doing each of the following prewriting and writing activities if you had 30 minutes to write your essay:

How much time would you spend…?

studying the exam question   _____

collecting information to include in your essay
(listing ideas, quickwriting, etc.)   _____

deciding how to organize your ideas (making an outline)   _____

writing your exam response   _____

checking grammar and spelling   _____

TOTAL   30 minutes

---

b. Make sure you understand the question you chose. Circle the important instruction words. Underline the important content words.

c. Collect information to answer the test question. List information you want to include in your answer. Quickwrite for several minutes in response to the question.

d. Make a rough outline identifying the points you want to include in your answer to the question. Think about the order in which you might present the information.

e. Come up with an organizer statement to begin your answer.

f. Write your answer in one page or less.

g. Read your essay response and ask yourself these questions:
- Did I answer the exam question?
- Is the information in my answer correct?
- Is my answer clear?
- Are there any grammar errors in my writing?

h. Ask a classmate or your teacher to tell you if you have answered the question correctly and clearly. (You don't have this option on a real exam.)

i. Put your writing in your writing folder.

Grammar Workshop 6a: parallel forms

1. Read the examples in the box and then answer the questions that follow.

> *Examples*
> - For years the Arabs **monopolized** the coffee trade and **prevented** the cultivation of coffee by other countries.
> - **Separating** the seeds from the rest of the fruit and **roasting** them are the most important steps in producing aromatic ground coffee.

    a. The boldfaced words in each sentence are "parallel in form." What do you think this means?

    b. Why do you think it's important to use parallel forms? *(Answers on page 160.)*

2. Rewrite the sentences below to make the underlined parts parallel to the rest of the sentence.

    a. Producing green tea involves picking the leaves, and bruising them to disrupt cell structure; <u>they are dried</u> quickly, and then <u>they are packaged</u>.

        Producing green tea involves picking the leaves, bruising them to disrupt cell structure, drying them quickly, and then packaging them.

    b. As caffeine circulates through the body, stomach acidity and urine output <u>are increased</u>, and caffeine causes a 10 percent rise in the metabolic rate.

        _____

        _____

    c. In the wet process of producing coffee, the fresh fruits are depulped by a machine and <u>a machine washes the seeds.</u>

        _____

        _____

    d. Producing aromatic ground coffee involves a number of steps: 1) selective hand picking of only the red, ripe berries; 2) <u>the berries are depulped and washed;</u> 3) fermenting the seeds; 4) <u>dry the beans;</u> and 5) <u>ships and trucks transport the green beans to market.</u>

        _____

        _____

        _____

Grammar Workshop 6b: conjunctive adverbs

1. Read the examples in the box and then answer the questions that follow.

Examples

- A tree's annual rings reflect each year's growth—from the spring when cells become large and divide, to the winter, when they stop dividing. **From the rings,** we can tell the approximate age of a tree.
- Diseases have invaded many plants that are native to the region. **For example,** in the 1950s, rye rust disease parasitized the rye plant.

   a. The **boldfaced** words are conjunctive adverbs or transitional words and phrases. What's the purpose of these words and phrases?

   b. What other conjunctive adverbs can you think of? *(Answers on page 160.)*

2. Underline the conjunctive adverb(s) in each set of sentences below.

   a. If a person is tired, caffeine makes that person more alert. In excessive doses, however, caffeine can produce unpleasant symptoms.

   b. For years the Arabs prevented the cultivation of coffee by other countries. Eventually, the Dutch managed to get live seeds from Mocha, a city in Yemen.

   c. The predominant use of *C. arabica* can be attributed to several of its characteristics. First, it is self-fertilizing and self-compatible. More importantly, however, coffee made from *C. arabica* has a better flavor than that made from the other two species.

3. What is the writer going to say next? Using the sentence in the box, write several possibilities using adverbs below.

Doctors now say that it isn't good to consume a lot of caffeine.

Conjunctive Adverbs

in other words	in addition	however	for this reason	in short
similarly	moreover	despite	thus	to summarize
that is	in the same way	above all	consequently	in conclusion

Example

Doctors now say that it isn't good to consume a lot of caffeine. However, fifty years ago they thought it was good for people.

Reporting on Research

Much academic writing consists of reporting on research. In this workshop, you will become more familiar with the format and organization of different types of research reports. You will then carry out a very short research assignment and report on it in writing.

1. Class Work. Study the information below and then answer the questions.

A laboratory report describes what happened during an experiment.

A research report describes how a research project was conducted, what the results were, and how the writer interprets the results.

A business report is a kind of financial progress report. It tells how a business is doing.

A progress report tells how far along you are in completing a task or project—what you have done and what you still need to do.

   a. What kinds of reports have you written?

   b. What kind of report might a historian write?

   c. In what professions might you have to write laboratory reports?

2. Pair Work. What might these people write a report about? For whom? List your ideas in the chart below.

	might write a report about	for (audience)
a high school math teacher	a student's progress in class	the student's parents
	a math project that worked well in class	other math teachers
the manager of a computer store		
a scientist studying acid rain		
an engineer in charge of a bridge-building project		

CRITICAL THINKING STRATEGY: *017 Applying What You Know* See page 146.

With your partner, write out your ideas in full sentences and share them with your classmates.

Example
A high school math teacher might write a report about a student's progress in class for the student's parents.

3. **On your own.** In some academic disciplines, you may be asked to use a specific format when you write a report. Some reports include the five sections listed below. What information would you include in each section? Choose from the list on the right.

CRITICAL THINKING STRATEGY:
018 Classifying
See page 148.

Information

	Sections
_b_ how I conducted my research	a) Introduction
____ explaining what I set out to do	b) Methodology
	c) Findings
____ how my findings might compare to the findings of others and/or what I might do with my findings	d) Analysis
	e) Conclusion
____ my interpretive report on the information I collected	
____ generalizations I can draw from my interpretations	

Compare ideas with your classmates.

4. **Group Work.** The report on pages 90–94 was written by a college student. Look over the report and answer the questions below.

READING STRATEGY:
010 Previewing
See page 136.

a. For this assignment, Michelle Graci, the writer of the report, had to choose a project that helped her to learn about language while providing a service to someone. Read the first paragraph of the report and then summarize her project in your own words.

b. How is the report organized?

c. If you were going to help Gilly, how would you go about it? What would you do?

Share ideas with the other groups in your class.

5. **On your own.** As you read the report on pages 90–96, write margin notes to help you read more actively.

READING STRATEGY:
015 Writing Margin Notes
See page 143.

disadvantaged because they have not mastered what has been set out as standard English.

It is also apparent to me that the kind of teaching we do in the schools needs to be reevaluated. The sink-or-swim approach is causing the loss of many brilliant young minds. We are all different. We learn in different ways and we all need different reinforcements. But we all need support, encouragement, and to feel we are worth the effort to learn and be taught.

I tried to give encouragement and support to Gilly. I can only hope that Gilly will continue in the forward motion he is now traveling. I realize his struggle is not over. I feel that if he continues to get help and support from me and others, he has a good chance at succeeding in his life.

We all have different backgrounds in language, and this has much to do with the way we perceive the world and the way the world reacts to us. Gilly is a good example of someone being judged harshly because of his lack of skill in language. Even I am guilty of some prejudice toward him. The first time I met him I perceived him as being slow. It did not take me long to see how wrong I was, and how wrong it is to stereotype people because of the way they use language. Gilly is a very bright boy. I did not make Gilly any smarter. I only started a change in the way society sees him and the way he sees himself.

Besides a change in Gilly, I am changing the way I approach teaching and people in general. Teaching is a big responsibility, but when approached with an open mind, tolerance, and the desire to enrich the lives of children, it is the most rewarding job. I believe I am going to love teaching.

References
Ryan, K. & Cooper, J.M. (1995). *Those who can, teach.* Boston: Houghton Mifflin Co.

Woolfolk, A. E. (1993). *Educational psychology.* Boston: Allyn and Bacon.

6. Pair Work. Compare margin notes with a partner. Then read the report again and take notes in the chart below.

⬛◆▦◆⬛◇▦⬛◆▦⬛◇

READING STRATEGY:
012 Taking Notes
See page 138.

Section	Important Points
Methodology	*got advice from a teacher*
	looked for information about learning styles in books
	_____
	_____
Findings	_____
	_____
	_____
	_____
Analysis	_____
	_____
	_____
	_____
Conclusion	_____
	_____
	_____
	_____

Compare charts with a partner.

CRITICAL THINKING STRATEGY
016 Analyzing
See page 144.

7. **Group Work.** Look at the report on pages 90–94 with a writer's eye. As you discuss the questions below, take turns recording your group's ideas.

   a. On a scale of 1 to 10 (with ten the highest), how interesting was this paper to you? Why?

   b. Who seems to be the audience for this report? Why do you think so?

   c. What were Graci's sources of information for this report?

   d. For this assignment, Michelle Graci had to choose a project that helped her to learn about language while providing a service to someone. What do you think was the most difficult part of this assignment? Why?

   Use your notes to report your group's ideas.

8. **Writing Assignment.** What are research reports in different academic fields like? For this writing assignment, you will collect information about the format and organization of a report or an article in an academic journal. You will then report your findings in writing to your classmates. Follow the steps below to get started.

   a. Look in a library for examples of professional or academic journals. Choose a journal in a field that interests you.

b. Look through the journal carefully and note answers to the questions below.

- How many reports or articles are included in this journal?

- In addition to reports and articles, what other kinds of writing are included in this journal? What is the purpose of each one?

- Choose one report or article. How is it organized? What headings does the writer use? Does it have subheadings? Is bibliographic information included? Does the writer quote other people?

Make notes about anything else in the journal that interests or surprises you.

c. If possible, get together with a classmate and report what you learned about the academic journal. Answer any questions your partner has.

d. Using the format below, write a two-page report telling your classmates about the journal you looked at. Explain what you learned about academic reports from this journal.

> ### Introduction
> What is your project? (Briefly describe it, acknowledging the assignment you were given.)
> What academic journal did you choose to study? Why?
> How did you find or know about this journal?
>
> ### Methodology
> How did you conduct your research?
> How did you collect information about the report or article?
>
> ### Findings
> What did you find out and what does it mean? (For example, how is the article organized and how does this help the reader?)
>
> ### Analysis
> What generalizations can you draw from your investigation? (For example, from this one journal, what can you say about academic reports in that academic field?)

> **Conclusion**
>
> How do your findings compare to the findings of some other classmates? (Interview several.)
>
> What can you do with what you have learned?

e. **Read Around.** Get together with several classmates. Take turns reading each other's paper. Write questions or comments in response to each person's paper.

f. Write one or more revised drafts of your report and place your writing in your writing folder.

⬛◆⬛⬛◆⬛⬛◆⬛⬛◆

WRITING STRATEGY:
006 Revising
See page 124.

Grammar Workshop 7: sentence variety

1. **Read the two paragraphs below and then answer the questions that follow.**

(1)

Developing a narrow focus helps ease the difficulty of writing a research paper. The smaller the idea, the more complex an issue can be. Lack of complexity is a common problem in inexperienced writing. Research papers at the college level are not meant to be acts of regurgitation, but development of thought based on a pool of information. The research part is the development of information. The writing is the thinking. Thinking comes much more naturally when the subject is something the writer really cares about.

(2)

A research paper can be difficult to develop. You can make it easier by developing a narrow focus. A small idea can deal with a more complex issue. A common problem in inexperienced writing is lack of complexity. Research papers at the college level are not meant to be acts of regurgitation. They are supposed to be a development of thought based on a pool of information. The research part is the development of information. The writing is the thinking. A writer who really cares about the subject will be able to think more naturally.

a. Which paragraph has more sentence variety? Give examples to explain your answer.

b. Which paragraph seems easier to follow? Why? *(Answers on page 161.)*

2. The paragraph below lacks sentence variety. Rewrite it to make it easier and more interesting to read.

(1)

    The way I study for essay exams is to first be sure I have read and understood all the required material. I must know all the information about the subject. I rewrite my notes on any key concepts the test might be about. I am getting into the habit of writing about things the test could cover. This helps to put me in essay mode.

(2)

Passing a Writing Test

At different times during your academic career you may have to take a test of your writing ability. The purpose of these tests is to find out how well you can communicate your ideas in writing. In this workshop, you will explore some of the criteria that instructors use to evaluate students' essays on a writing test. You will also look at some sample writing test responses and have the chance to take several practice tests.

1. Pair Work. Ask your partner the questions below. Write down your partner's answers.

Questions	Answers
a. When did you last take a writing test?	
b. Do you remember the writing prompt?	
c. How much time did you have to write your essay?	
d. Did you know the writing prompt in advance?	
e. What was done with the results?	

Get together with another pair and report your partner's answers.
What similarities do you find among the answers?

CRITICAL THINKING STRATEGY: *016 Analyzing* See page 144.

2. On your own. The essay on page 103 is one student's response on a writing test. This writer had *thirty minutes* to choose from a list of writing prompts and write a short essay. Read the essay several times and answer the questions below.

a. What is the purpose of each paragraph in the essay?

Paragraph #	Purpose
1	_____
2	_____
3	_____
4	_____

b. The writer explores two questions in this essay. What is the second question she answers?

Question 1: What force has contributed most significantly to your development?

Answer: Having my father in my life.

Question 2: _____

Answer: He taught me to love books, and he influenced my thinking about God.

Get together with several classmates and compare ideas.

102

Sample Writing Test Response #1

The force that has contributed most significantly to my development is my father. My parents were divorced while I was very young, and it was decided that I should live with my mother. That might make you think that my father had little to do with my upbringing, but through the years he has guided me at every turn. He visits me often and we talk a great deal. Although he has influenced me in many ways, both large and small, two of these seem most significant to me.

Because of my father, I love books. He always gives me books to read that will give me something to think about. His latest gift is a book entitled *We*, a story about an anonymous number in a communist society, which has changed my whole view of that particular social system. *A Clockwork Orange* and *The Hitchhiker's Guide to the Galaxy*, both gifts from my father, have also contributed to my thinking.

My father has also influenced my thinking about God. Neither of us believes in the existence of one true God. That thinking is too generic, and one God could not possibly fill the needs of everyone. My father and I believe in a personal god, or rather, we believe in the idea that each person has a personal god. Even people who believe in one God see that one God in different ways, making uniformity impossible.

My father has influenced me in different ways. I hope that I can become like him, and he says the same about me.

CRITICAL THINKING
STRATEGY:
016 Analyzing
See page 144.

3. **Group Work.** Below is another student's response to the same writing test prompt. This response illustrates a common writing problem. Read this essay and answer the questions that follow.

Writing Prompt
Discuss the force or forces that have contributed most significantly to your development.

Sample Writing Test Response #2

Music is the force that has contributed most significantly to my development. The emotion music expresses makes it significant to me. Writing and playing music are ways I vent frustration and anger. When I play my bass guitar, my emotions flow through it. When listening to music, especially live music, I can hear what the musician is feeling, and I can feel what he feels. Through music, I can bring out emotions and share feelings which I normally cannot bring out and share. Listening to blues, I can hear sorrows and depressions in every whine of the harp and every lick of the guitar. Listening to a jazz musician solo, I can hear the anger and brutality coming from the crunching, bottom-ended, distorted guitar and the driving double bass drums. Music is a driving force behind my development and has helped me to channel my feelings and emotions into something creative and artistic.

---

a. How is this essay different from the essay on page 103?

b. What different choices did these two writers make?

c. Why does Writing Test Response #1 seem easier to follow?

d. What suggestions would you give the writer of Response #2?

4. **Group Work.** The list below shows the criteria that a teacher might use to evaluate a *thirty-minute* writing test. Use these criteria to evaluate the essays on pages 103 and 104. For each criterion, assign a point value from 5 (excellent) to 1 (poor). Be prepared to give reasons and examples to support your evaluation.

CRITICAL THINKING STRATEGY: *020 Evaluating* See page 153.

	Response #1 (page 103)	Response #2 (page 104)
• The essay has a clear focus.	_____	_____
• Ideas get developed.	_____	_____
• Examples and details support the writer's ideas.	_____	_____
• The reader perceives the writing to be coherent.	_____	_____
• Sentence structure is varied.	_____	_____
• Grammar is acceptable.	_____	_____

Compare ideas with the other groups in your class.

5. **Pair Work.** Below are some typical prompts for a writing test. To find a focus for your writing, try pulling questions from the prompts. Remember to come up with questions you can answer in thirty minutes. The first one is done for you. The second is partially complete.

WRITING STRATEGY: *002 Making Your Thesis Clear* See page 117.

Writing Prompt #1: In one to two pages, explore a childhood experience that changed your life in some way.

What childhood experience changed my life in some way?

How did this experience change my life?

Writing Prompt #2: Argue for or against a government crackdown on cigarette advertising.

Should or shouldn't the government crack down on cigarette advertising?

_____

_____

Writing Prompt #3: In one to two pages, explore ways to stay healthy.

_____

_____

_____

_____

Writing Prompt #4: What are the most important reasons for getting a university education? (Note: Because this writing prompt is already in the form of a question, you need only come up with one more question to focus your writing.)

_____

_____

Writing Prompt #5: My Favorite Leisure Activities

_____

_____

_____

_____

Writing Prompt #6: What I Would Do If I Had Only Six Months to Live

_____

_____

_____

_____

Share ideas with your classmates.

6. **On your own.** The chart below lists some of the things you need to do when you are taking a writing test. On a *thirty-minute* writing test, how would you divide up your time? For each activity below, write the amount of time.

> ### *How much time would you spend…?*
>
> deciding how to focus the topic _____
>
> collecting ideas to include in your essay
> (listing ideas, quickwriting, etc.) _____
>
> deciding how to organize your ideas _____
>
> writing your essay _____
>
> checking grammar and spelling _____
>
> _____
>
> TOTAL 30 minutes

Compare ideas with your classmates.

7. **Writing Assignment.** Choose one of the writing prompts in Activity 5 and give yourself thirty minutes to write a response. Remember to plan how you will use the thirty minutes, using the chart above.

8. **Pair Work.** Exchange essays with your partner. Read your partner's essay and then answer the questions below.

• What questions does the writer answer in this essay? (Write the questions at the bottom of your partner's paper.)

• What seems to be the purpose of each paragraph in your partner's essay? (Write your ideas in the margin of your partner's paper.)

Return your partner's paper with your comments. Read your partner's comments on your own paper and then list 3 things you would like to do to improve your essay.

9. **On your own.** Ask your teacher or another classmate to evaluate your essay, using the criteria below. Then place it in your writing folder.

	YES	Needs more work.
• The essay has a clear focus.	_____	_____
• Ideas get developed.	_____	_____
• Examples and details support the writer's ideas.	_____	_____
• The reader perceives the writing to be coherent.	_____	_____
• Sentence structure is varied.	_____	_____
• Grammar is acceptable.	_____	_____

10. **Pair Work.** The essay on pages 109–110 is another student's response on a writing test. For this test, however, the writer had *two hours* to write an essay. Read this essay several times and answer the questions below.

a. How did the writer focus the writing prompt? What questions did he answer in his essay? Add to the list below.

Question: What experience changed your attitude about something or someone?

Answer: The time a good friend lied and stole from me.

Question: So this experience changed your attitude. What about?

Answer: Friendship.

Question: How did your attitude about friendship change?

Answer: _____

b. When you have two hours to write an essay instead of thirty minutes, your evaluator will expect a more developed piece of writing. In what ways is this essay more developed than the essays on pages 103 and 104?

Share ideas with your classmates.

Writing Prompt
Write about an experience that changed your attitude about something or someone.

Sample Writing Test Response #3

How I Lost a Friend

People say that friendship is something very important, maybe the most important thing in the world. They also say that even today when money is everything, friendship is still crucial. For me, friendship is something very important too, and I can say that I have friends for whom I would do anything. However, there is another side of friendship about which I would like to write now, and show you how with lying, slandering, and stealing, a best friend can become an enemy. To be more specific, I will tell you how I lost a friend.

I had a friend who I had known for a long, long time. He was my best friend and business partner. Together we had a great time and great success in business, because we trusted each other. But one day I discovered that he was stealing money from our company. When he needed money for clothes, he just took from the company's account and when he went to a disco or pub, he paid with the firm's credit card, not with his own card. He did this not because he needed money but because he was stingy. And I can say that this was crucial for our friendship and maybe the first step of losing him as a friend.

The other thing that destroyed our friendship was that he lied to me. When I discovered that money was missing, I asked him if he knew where it was. He said that he didn't know; he said that he would never steal money from the business. Can you imagine how I felt? And that was the point. He looked me in the eye and lied without thinking, without any shame. I couldn't forgive him for that because I had trusted him and I had considered him to be my best friend.

The last thing that contributed to ruining our friendship was his slandering of me. He told our friends that I didn't know anything about business and that the firm was going badly because of my poor knowledge of bargaining. Also, he said that I was the person who was going to pubs and having fun, not him. The worst thing about all this slandering was that my friends began thinking that I was a terrible person. The consequence was that for a while I lost many good friends. For a while I was alone; no one trusted me.

In the end you see how a best friend who you have known for a long time can become your enemy. And I can say that after this case I completely changed my notion about friendship. However, that doesn't mean that I don't have friends anymore. On the contrary, I still have my best friends, but I just think that I will never trust them as I did before. For this kind of case, in my country we have a saying which is "Please Lord, protect me from my friends. I can protect myself from my enemies." As you see, it is difficult to find really good friends. Even if you have know them for a long time, sometimes that doesn't mean that you can trust them. And the only thing that I can suggest to you is to be careful when you trust your friends. Always be prepared for surprises.

—Kiril Milanov
Student, University of New Orleans

CRITICAL THINKING STRATEGY:
016 Analyzing
See page 144.

11. **Group Work.** Work together to answer the questions below.

   a. In his essay, Kiril Milanov both describes a personal experience and gives his interpretation of it. Look back at his essay and find a sentence in which he gives an interpretation.

   b. Milanov tells a personal story and yet he also connects this story to a larger issue. What is the larger issue?

   c. An evaluator might say that Milanov's essay shows "an awareness of audience." What do you think this means?

   d. In the text on the next page, Milanov's interpretations and analyses have been removed. Do you think the essay still shows an awareness of audience? Why or why not?

I had a friend who I had known for a long, long time. He was my best friend and business partner. Together we had a great time and great success in business, because we trusted each other. But one day I discovered that he was stealing money from our company. When he needed money for clothes, he just took from the company's account and when he went to a disco or pub, he paid with the firm's credit card, not with his own card. He did this not because he needed money but because he was stingy.

When I discovered that money was missing, I asked him if he knew where it was. He said that he didn't know; he said that he would never steal money from the business. He looked me in the eye and lied without thinking, without any shame.

He told our friends that I didn't know anything about business and that the firm was going badly because of my poor knowledge of bargaining. Also, he said that I was the person who was going to pubs and having fun, not him. The worst thing about all this slandering was that my friends began thinking that I was a terrible person. The consequence was that for a while I lost many good friends. For a while I was alone; no one trusted me.

Share answers with the other groups in your class.

12. **Group Work.** The list at the top of the next page shows the criteria that an evaluator might use to evaluate a *two-hour* writing test. Use these criteria to evaluate the essay on pages 109–110. For each criterion, assign a point value from 5 (excellent) to 1 (poor). Be prepared to give reasons and examples to support your evaluation.

CRITICAL THINKING
STRATEGY:
020 Evaluating
See page 153.

> ***Writing Test Response #3***
>
> It has a beginning, middle, and end. _____
>
> There is a stated or implied thesis. _____
>
> Sentence structure is varied. _____
>
> The reader perceives the writing to be coherent. _____
>
> Examples and details support the writer's ideas. _____
>
> The writer gets beyond description. _____
>
> The writer makes a point. _____

Compare ideas with the other groups in your class.

13. **On your own.** The chart below lists some of the things you need to do when you are taking a long writing test. How would you divide up *two hours?* For each activity, write the amount of time.

> ***How much time would you spend…?***
>
> deciding how to focus the topic _____
>
> making an outline or diagram to figure _____
> out how to organize your ideas
>
> thinking of and listing examples and _____
> details to support your idea
>
> writing your essay _____
>
> rewriting and rearranging to _____
> improve the flow of ideas
>
> checking grammar and spelling _____
> _____
>
> TOTAL   120 minutes

Compare plans with your classmates.

14. Writing Assignment. Choose from the list of writing prompts below. Then give yourself *two hours* to write your essay, following steps a–f below. Remember to plan your time, using the information in the chart in Activity 13.

> ### Writing Prompts
>
> - Write about an experience that changed your attitude about something/someone.
>
> - Discuss the force or forces that have contributed most significantly to your development.
>
> - What the word "courage" means to me
>
> - Ways to Stay Healthy
>
> - My Favorite Holiday / Relative / Book, etc.
>
> - Write about the effects of the women's movement.
>
> - Discuss how advertising affects our lives.
>
> - Honesty is/is not the best policy.

a. Make sure you understand the writing prompt.

b. To find a focus for your writing, try pulling questions from the writing prompt. Write them down. Then quickwrite in response to your questions.

c. Look over your quickwriting to find a topic to write about. Remember that you will need to do more than report information or tell a story. What larger issue can you raise?

d. Brainstorm information (examples and details) to use in your writing.

e. Think about how you might organize your ideas. Try writing a rough draft or outline of your essay to help you organize your ideas. Experiment with different ways to present your ideas.

f. Write your essay.

❖ **Why is it important to cite your sources?**

As a college writer, you are expected to work with other people's ideas and "weave" them into your writing. There are several reasons for this:

    a. to show that your writing is public (part of the "marketplace" of ideas)

    b. to strengthen your ideas by showing that experts agree

    c. to demonstrate that you have done your homework.

❖ **Caution!**

Others people's words and ideas cannot replace your own. So, don't rely too heavily on others' words. Think of the proper balance as a kind of equation:

Your ideas and words: at least 75%
Others' work: less than 25%

You can't let others speak *for you*. Instead, use their ideas to introduce, develop, or support your own.

❖ **Examples of citing sources**

    a. Leon Lederman, a Nobel Prize-winning scientist, credits dedication and imagination for his success (*Christian Science Monitor,* 1989). Lederman is not the only…

    b. "We want to keep our environment pure and clean," says Edward Cornish, president of World Future Society, a group that studies sociological and technological trends (quoted by Sit, *The Boston Globe Career Guide,* 1992). Jobs in environmental preservation will be in demand, according to Cornish.

    c. According to Judson Landis, a sociologist, parents act differently towards their children based on their gender (*Sociology,* 1992).

    d. In the short story "Who's Hu?," a young Chinese immigrant discovers that American girls aren't supposed to be good in math (Namioka, 1993). This is only one kind of gender stereotyping that exists in American society.

   e. Immigrant children adapt to their new linguistic and cultural "landscapes" in very different ways, sometimes even enduring years of miserable silence. (See Hong Kingston, 1975.)

   f. "Who should I marry?" Ah, that is a question, perhaps *the* question, we each ask ourselves. Maybe the answer is dictated by our parents. Or perhaps it is offered as advice, as it was when Gary Soto's grandmother told him to marry a Mexican girl (1986). Whoever we marry, though, one researcher says that one point is clear: we should marry someone like ourselves (Drexler, 1993).

[Note: Examples a–c give more information than is necessary if a bibliography were going to be added. Examples d–f assume the addition of a bibliography.]

❖ Additional advice

Document others' ideas, whether or not you write their exact words. Even if you put their ideas into your words, the ideas are still someone else's. You have to document the source.

Look up 004 Paraphrasing (p. 121) and 008 Using Quotations (p. 129) for more help.

---

002 MAKING YOUR THESIS CLEAR

❖ Thesis: What? and Why?

A thesis is an organizing idea for writing. For example, do you want to develop your writing around "the secret to a successful marriage"? Around "the big question of who you should marry"? A good thesis can provide a framework for your paper.

Before you write, working out a thesis and shaping it into a sentence can get you started. It can help you think about your topic and plan how to develop it. Remember, though, a thesis sentence is a tool, *not* an introduction.

Writers may or may not state their thesis directly. Keep in mind, though, that you must have a controlling idea in order to write coherently, and that it needs to be clear to your readers, whether or not you state it directly.

❖ Ways to state a thesis

a. State it directly

The Secrets of Marital Bliss

   Sometimes camouflaged in the dense lingo of academia are the plain facts we need to run our lives. What, for instance, is the secret of a happy marriage? Not surprise gourmet meals, getaway weekends, or other nostrums dispensed in women's magazines. Rather, according to one researcher, the secret of marital bliss resides in a simple notion: positive assortative mating. Translation: Marry someone like yourself.

(Drexler, The Boston Globe, 1993)

[Note: The rest of the article—eight paragraphs—explains and details the idea of "similarity" as a strengthening dimension of marriage.]

b. State it indirectly

Like Mexicans

   My grandmother gave me bad advice and good advice when I was in my early teens. For the bad advice, she said I should become a barber because they made good money and listened to the radio all day. …For the good advice, she said I should marry a Mexican girl. …We went in the living room where she lectured me on the virtues of the Mexican girl: first, she could cook and, second, she acted like a woman, not a man, in her husband's home. She said she would tell me about a third when I got a little older.

[Paragraph 6] But the woman I married was not Mexican but Japanese. It was a surprise to me. …

[Paragraph 8] I was in love and there was no looking back. She was the one. …I told my mother, who was slapping hamburgers into patties. "Well, sure if you want to marry her," she said. But the more I talked, the more concerned she became. Later I began to worry. Was it all a mistake? "Marry a Mexican girl," I heard my mother say in my mind. …

[Paragraph 9] I worried about it until Carolyn took me home to meet her parents. …

[Paragraph 13, after visiting Carolyn's parents]…I looked back, waving… Like Mexicans, I thought. …On the highway, I felt happy, pleased by it all. …Her people were like Mexicans, only different (Soto, 1986).

[Note: Although the writer does not directly state his thesis as a direct assertion, he never strays from his controlling idea, which is an answer to the question "Who should I marry?"]

For a reader's perspective on a thesis, see 009 Identifying the Writer's Thesis (p. 133).

---

003 ORGANIZING IDEAS

❖ When to organize?

Writers work in different ways. Some writers prefer to organize their ideas before they start writing. Some prefer to get started by quickwriting, see what ideas emerge, and then (re)organize them later. (See 005 Quickwriting.) Others prefer to brainstorm, jotting down ideas, and organizing those they like later. Which do you prefer?

❖ Strategies for organizing ideas before you write

a. Taking notes in a chart is a good way to collect and organize ideas for writing. To make a chart, think about the kinds of information you want to organize. List this information as headings in your chart. Then add ideas and examples under each heading.

Example:

Field of Work	Jobs Available	Reasons for Growth in Jobs
health care	nurse	population growing older
education	teacher	children of baby boomers reaching school age
financial services	accountant	more reliance on information

b. Outline your general plan for writing. This is a good way to organize your ideas. Keep in mind, though, that your outline is *only* a plan. New ideas may emerge as you write, and you can change your mind at any time.

Example of an outline:

I. Controlling idea (thesis): Family traditions are important to children's emotional well-being.

Reasons why:

• Traditions give children a sense of belonging.

• Traditions help them create an identity.

II. Develop first reason: Why do traditions give children a sense of belonging?

• Tell about my own family traditions

• Cite Sandra Cisneros, what she says about her Mexican-American heritage

III. Develop second reason: Why do traditions help children create an identity?

• Cite Amy Tan, from *The Joy Luck Club*

IV. Conclusion

• For readers to think about: What can be done to support the efforts of immigrant parents to maintain their language and culture? One suggestion: art and drama programs, run by members of the local community

c. Write out your thesis or controlling idea. A thesis statement is really an organizing tool. It expresses your organizing idea for writing.

Example of a thesis statement:

> Family traditions help a child establish a positive identity and a sense of belonging.

d. Choose a "working" title to help you organize and focus your ideas. You can change the title later if your thinking evolves in a different direction, or a better title comes to mind.

e. Make a modified outline of your general plan for writing, more in the form of reminder notes.

Example of a modified outline:

> Introduction (to a movie review): Identify the movie by title and director. Briefly tell the story plot; identify actors by their roles.

> Body: Give my evaluation of the movie—how well the plot works, how well it's acted, how well it's directed, what the message of the movie is, etc. Include examples to show what I mean.

> Conclusion: Summarize my review. Tell movie-goers if they should spend their money to see the film.

[Note: The divisions here do not necessarily "translate" into paragraphs. A very short review, for instance, might be no more than one paragraph altogether.]

---
004 PARAPHRASING

❖ **What? and When?**

Paraphrasing is rewriting somebody else's idea, only using different words. If you use someone's *exact* words, you are quoting, *not* paraphrasing; and the words must be "surrounded" by quotation marks (or put in *italics,* if you are word-processing).

When paraphrasing someone else's words, use your words. In other words, write the thought the way you would express it. But here's the tricky part: putting others' ideas into your own words does not give you "ownership." *The ideas are still someone else's.* So, you still have to document your source.

❖ Example of paraphrasing vs. quoting

a. Original text

> When I went to kindergarten and had to speak English for the first time, I became silent… (p. 170). During the first silent year I spoke to no one at school, did not ask before going to the lavatory, and flunked kindergarten. My sister also said nothing for three years, silent in the playground and silent at lunch… (p. 171).
>
> (Kingston, 1975; in Blanton/Lee, 1995)

b. Quoting from the original text

> Each year thousands of children immigrate to the United States. These children face the daunting task of learning to live in two different worlds—the home world and the public world—each with its own culture and language. Each child evolves his/her own way of managing the task. Maxine Hong Kingston, for example, responded with silence (1975; in Blanton/Lee, 1995). She **"spoke to no one at school, did not ask before going to the lavatory, and flunked kindergarten"** (p. 171). Her sister **"also said nothing for three years"** (p. 171).

c. Paraphrasing from the original text

> Growing up as immigrants in a new country can be confusing for children. They are faced with learning to live in two different worlds, each with its own culture and language. Each child finds his/her own way of coping. Take Maxine Hong Kingston, for example. **She responded with three years of silence, as did her sister** (1975; in Blanton/Lee, 1995, pp. 170–71).

005 QUICKWRITING

❖ Why? and When?

Quickwriting, or freewriting, is a useful way to collect ideas for writing. Think of it as tapping into your conscious and subconscious mind. The point is to get your brain moving. Quickwrite when getting started, or anytime you get stuck.

❖ Steps to follow

1. Choose a topic—something to write about.

2. For 10–15 minutes, write quickly. Put down anything that comes to mind. Put it down, even if it turns out to be garbage that you'll discard later.

3. Don't worry about grammar or spelling. Don't even worry about writing full sentences. If you can't think of a word in English, write it in another language, or leave a blank. The trick is to write without stopping.

4. If you can't think of anything to write, put that down or write the same word over and over again. Keep your pen or pencil moving.

5. When you finish writing, read over your ideas. Circle the ones you might want to keep. If you see a controlling idea emerging, try writing it out in a summary sentence. Or write it out as a summary idea.

❖ Example of quickwriting

Writing topic: Growing old

I'm not looking forward to growing old. Is anyone? I think about my grandmother and how difficult her life is. She's 93 now. Many of her friends are dead. Hmmm, what else? Oh, yes, she complains about the things she can't do so well anymore. Trouble walking. Can't hear very well. But she says she feels young inside. That seems xxxxxxxxx. Bizarre. Is that the word I want? I always thought if you were old, you felt old. For some people, maybe it's just the body that ages. I can't think of anything to write. I can't think of anything to write. Grandmother's body is getting old, but her mind is young. She reads all of the time, and she still likes to try new things. She's learning to paint. She actually signed up for a painting class at that place on Magazine Street—what's the name of it? She's excited about that....

Summary idea: *old in body, young in spirit*

For use of quickwriting as a reading strategy, see 011 Quickwriting (p.136).

006 REVISING

❖ What?

"Revising" literally means "seeing again." Think of revising as a process for developing your writing, not simply as a way to correct it. Revising "happens" at many different times during writing. And the process may change from person to person.

Some people revise in their heads before they even start drafting. Others may begin the drafting process by quickwriting, without any concern for making changes, and then work from a rough draft to "re-see" their ideas and decide where to go, what to keep, and how to focus their writing.

❖ Revising, editing, and proofreading are different!

Revising is more basic than *editing*, which involves rearranging ideas and sentences, and perhaps deleting some. Editing happens after the writer pretty much has everything down on paper.

Revising is much more basic than *proofreading*, which involves re-reading everything one last time (or so the writer hopes!) to make sure that all the little things, such as spelling and punctuation, are correct.

❖ Revising as a process

Although writers each have their own way of revising, revision is always *recursive*, meaning that it goes back and forth, back and forth, again and again. It always involves (re)thinking, (re)reading, and (re)writing.

Although there are no formulae for successful revising and no simple 1-2-3 steps to follow, the revising process might "look" something like this:

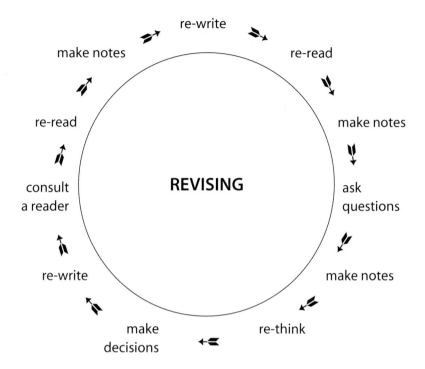

As a writer, you might repeat any part of the process a number of times before you are satisfied with your work.

❖ Ask fundamental questions

Fundamental to revising are these questions:

> Who is my audience?
>
> What is my relationship to them?
>
> What do they need to know?
>
> Why do they need to hear it from me?

Based on your answers, you can decide on your topic, choose the points you want to make, know which kinds of examples and illustrations might help your audience understand, and figure out the tone of voice you want to build into your writing (friendly? businesslike? formal? etc.).

❖ Remember the terms of the assignment

In college writing, you can't forget the assignment itself. Is it a 2–3 page essay? A 5–6 page research report? The context of the class and your understanding of the teacher's expectations and requirements strongly influence your writing. For example, are you required to use headings to organize your writing, as in the research report on pages 90–94? Be sure you understand the assignment.

❖ Using a checklist

As you write, you may want to think along the lines indicated in the checklist (next page) to formulate your ideas, write, read your writing, and reformulate and rewrite. You can't revise for everything at once, so take each of the groups of questions one at a time. Of course, polishing your ideas comes last; that is more a part of editing and even proof-reading.

Your classmates could also use the checklist to give you feedback on your writing. And your teacher might use it to evaluate the final draft. As is, the checklist is especially valuable as a guide to writing essays.

❖ Revising the checklist

For revising research reports and other documents for science and business courses, you might need to modify the checklist slightly. For instance, you might add a section like this:

Meeting discipline-specific expectations:

- Does the writing express the tone my audience expects?
- Does the format (sections, headings, etc.) include all that my audience expects?
- Does my writing sound and appear "professional"?
- Is the information correct?
- Are my sources documented?

Checklist for Revising

Yes ✓

	First draft	Second draft	Third draft	Final draft

Sharpening your focus

- Is it clear who the audience is? ❏ ❏ ❏ ❏
- Is the topic limited enough? ❏ ❏ ❏ ❏
- Have unnecessary words been deleted? ❏ ❏ ❏ ❏

Making your writing interesting

- Does the introduction "hook" the reader? ❏ ❏ ❏ ❏
- Does the writer use interesting details? ❏ ❏ ❏ ❏
- Does the writer's voice come through? ❏ ❏ ❏ ❏

Helping your reader follow your ideas

- Does the title suggest the writer's thinking? ❏ ❏ ❏ ❏
- Does the introduction guide the reader? ❏ ❏ ❏ ❏
- Can the reader perceive the writer's plan? ❏ ❏ ❏ ❏

Polishing your ideas

- Do the sentences vary in length? ❏ ❏ ❏ ❏
- Are the ideas connected? ❏ ❏ ❏ ❏
- Are the verb forms and tenses correct? ❏ ❏ ❏ ❏
- Are the punctuation and spelling correct? ❏ ❏ ❏ ❏

007 SUMMARIZING

❖ What? and How?

A summary gives the main points. It is a compact, condensed version of the original. To summarize, don't work from the original text. Instead, work from your own head. Write from your understanding of the main ideas, without copying from the original text.

❖ Example of summarizing

Original paragraph:

Rosa Parks

Thirty-six years ago, on a bus in Montgomery, Alabama, Rosa Parks refused to give up her seat to a white man, defying a Southern tradition of decades. To appreciate that act, we have to remember that the mid-1950s were a time when the Ku Klux Klan was in its heyday, when the 1954 Supreme Court ruling against segregation in the schools had fanned the bigotry of white supremacists, and when lynchings of blacks in the Deep South were being widely reported. If the precise moment of the birth of the Civil Rights movement can be isolated, it may be said that it was from this one woman's singular act of courage.   (Excerpted from Ragghianti, *Parade Magazine*, 1992)

Summary of original:

In a simple act of courage, Rosa Parks refused to give up her bus seat to a white man, and thus began the U.S. Civil Rights movement. The year was 1956; the place, Montgomery, Alabama (Ragghianti, 1992).

❖ How to write a summary

a. Somewhere—at the beginning or the end—reference the source: (title), author, date. At the beginning, you may also want to identify the genre (article, interview, short story, etc.).

b. Include the main ideas and key points.

c. Condense the ideas into a fraction of the original length. If your summary is longer than, say, a quarter of the original, you are probably including too many details.

d. Write from your own understanding: this is what is meant by "use your own words."

❖ **Reasons to write a summary**

   a. To check your own reading comprehension. After you read something, try summarizing it. If you have trouble, go back and read it again.

   b. To write a review of a film or book. Incorporate a brief summary of the contents before you interpret and evaluate the work.

   c. To analyze a poem, story, or other work of literature. Summarize it before you launch into your analysis.

   d. To research a topic for a paper or other course assignment. This is a form of note taking. Remember to record the (a) title of the article, (b) author, (c) book or journal in which it appears, (d) date of publication or volume number, (e) place of publication, if a book, (f) name of editor, if an edited volume, and (g) page numbers of the material you are summarizing.

   e. To present your plan for a research project. This is called a *promissory summary* or *abstract*. Include the (a) topic, (b) key points you plan to make, and (c) titles of books, journals, or other sources you plan to consult. If you are assigned this kind of summary, ask the teacher for a model to guide you in writing your own.

   f. To "prove" that you have read and understood the assignment. Some teachers will ask for a *reading summary,* often followed by a short piece of writing connecting the topic and ideas to yourself. In effect, you have to write a kind of essay: first, summarize the reading; then, relate it to your prior learning and experience. If a teacher assigns a reading summary, ask for guidelines or a sample.

008 USING QUOTATIONS

❖ **Reasons to quote**

In college writing, you are expected to work "across texts," as you enter "conversations" about ideas. This means pulling ideas and information from other texts (essays, articles, etc.) into your own emerging text. You can do this either directly, as quotations, or indirectly, as a rephrasing of what someone said. (See also 004 Paraphrasing.)

   Incorporating others' research and ideas gives your writing a sense of "authority." After all, you are an expert, if you find experts who think like you. Even when they think differently, you come across as an expert as long as you explain the difference and use it to your advantage.

You may also be given assignments that require you to report on someone else's research. This is different from using others' ideas to support your own. In the case of reporting on someone else's research, it may not be appropriate to express your own opinion about it. Your job might then be to present "just the facts."

❖ **Caution when using others' words to support your ideas!**

To quote successfully, you need to achieve balance between your thoughts and someone else's. Think of balance as a kind of equation:

YOU: at least 75%
OTHERS: less than 25%

Others' ideas should not replace your own; other people cannot speak for you. Rather, use their ideas to develop and support your ideas. Your ideas should occupy the foreground, so to speak; their ideas—if they serve to explain, support, or introduce yours—occupy the background.

a. Example of quoting too much

> **Mohandas K. Gandhi**
>
> "Mohandas Gandhi is revered by Indians as the founder of their nation" (Barash, 1991, p. 94). Gandhi accomplished his goal to bring freedom to India. "He also showed that a highly spiritual concept—nonviolence—can be an intensely practical tool in the quest for peace, even in the twentieth-century world of…power, and violence" (p. 97).

b. Example of proper balance

> **Making a Difference**
>
> Can one person make a difference? I certainly have never thought that *I* could change the world. Yet, if we take a lesson from history, we find that one person can indeed make a lasting difference. Take the great teacher Gandhi, for example. He accomplished his goal of bringing freedom to the people of India. From him, millions also learned nonviolent resistance as both an **"approach to life and an intensely practical technique of achieving political and social change"** (Barash, 1991, p. 94). From Gandhi, Martin Luther King, Jr. learned the lessons he needed to create a movement for social and political change in the United States. Gandhi's life and teachings have truly changed the world.

❖ **Opening your writing with a quotation**

Introductions are often difficult to write. Try using a quotation; it can serve as a good opening. The trick, though, is to find exactly the right quotation—one that is interesting, will attract your readers, and lead directly into your topic.

Example of opening with a quotation:

> Intelligent—and Illiterate
>
> "I just felt dumb. And dumb was how the kids treated me. They'd make fun of me every chance they got, asking me to spell 'cat' or something like that. Even if I knew how to spell it, I wouldn't; they'd only give me another word. Anyway, it was awful, because more than anything I wanted friends" (*The New York Times*, 1976). So writes David Raymond, a seventeen-year-old high school student, about growing up with dyslexia and the difficulties he had learning to read…

[Note: The essay continues, defining dyslexia, explaining its effects on a child's learning, and offering remedies that seem to work in helping dyslexic children to learn to read.]

❖ **Punctuating quotations**

a. Put quotation marks around the writer's exact words.

Example:

> "Gandhi was born in India, in 1869; his parents were merchant-caste Hindus," writes David Barash, in *Introduction to Peace Studies* (1991).

b. Use a capital letter to begin a full comment, even if the comment begins in the middle of a sentence:

Example:

> According to David Barash, author of *Introduction to Peace Studies* (1991), "Central to Gandhi's world view was the search for truth."
>
> **But:** "Central to Gandhi's world view," reports David Barash (1991), "was the search for truth."

c. Use a comma, question mark, or exclamation point—whichever is appropriate—to separate the exact words being quoted from the rest of the sentence.

Example:

> "Gandhi was deeply grieved by the intense periodic violence between Hindus and Moslems," says David Barash, in his textbook *Introduction to Peace Studies* (1991).

d. Put periods and commas inside (to the left of) the second quotation mark.

Example:

> 1. "Gandhi was a small, slight man with indomitable moral certitude and remarkable physical stamina," writes David Barash (1991).
>
> 2. David Barash (1991) claims that "Gandhi was a small, slight man with indomitable moral certitude and remarkable physical stamina."

❖ **Quoting directly or indirectly?**

a. Example of a direct quotation

> "The traditions I grew up with gave me a security greater than money could ever buy," says Tencha Avila, a writer who grew up in a Mexican-American family (*Hispanic Magazine,* 1983). I too was given traditions more valuable than money. From my Moroccan grandparents, I learned…

b. Example of an indirect quotation

> According to John Tepper Marlin, author of "The Best Places in the U.S." (*Parade Magazine,* 1992) the best place to make money is New York City. My experience there tells me otherwise. For me, New York City was a complete financial disaster.…

READING STRATEGIES

009 IDENTIFYING THE WRITER'S THESIS

❖ What is a thesis?

A thesis is a writer's organizing idea for writing. The thesis of a text is more than just its topic. It is the topic, *plus* what the writer thinks about it, or even does with it. In successful writing, all the ideas, examples, and details relate to the writer's thesis.

❖ The reader as detective

Like a good detective, a reader starts looking for clues to the writer's thesis immediately. (See 010 Previewing, p. 136.) Notice the title, pictures or any other visuals, and subheadings—from these, you begin to answer the question *What's going on here?* Then, zero in on the first few lines, or first few paragraphs, to see if the writer tells you directly or indirectly what's going on.

❖ Getting inside the writer's head

Just as a successful writer must construct a framework around a central idea, you have to (re)construct the framework for a successful reading. This means getting inside the writer's head. To do that, look for direct thesis sentences, organizer statements, or purpose statements.

❖ Direct thesis statements

In a short piece of writing, look for an actual *thesis statement,* that is, a single sentence declaring what the writer plans to "prove."

   a. Example of a direct statement:

   Wearing seat belts saves lives.

In a very short essay (2–3 pages), this statement traditionally appears near the end of the introduction (first or second paragraph). If you sense that everything at the beginning of a text is leading toward a single declaration, then you are probably on the trail of a thesis statement.

b. Example of a thesis directly stated

Resisting the Forces That Pull Couples Apart

For the first time, researchers are arriving at a consensus on what it takes for a marriage to survive. Like the ingredients of successful marriages themselves, the findings are often surprising.

There is now strong evidence that the relationships most likely to end in divorce are not necessarily those in which spouses fight, passionately or often. Nor are married couples who have agreed to avoid conflict invariably headed for trouble, as previous research had suggested.

Rather, the latest studies suggest that **the marriages most likely to dissolve are those in which some or all of these four behaviors are chronic: criticism, contempt, defensiveness, and withdrawal.** Psychologist John Gottman, along with several other respected researchers in the field, have found that these are the strongest predictors of separation and divorce...

(Bass, 1993, *The Boston Globe*)

[Note: The article continues for 13 more paragraphs, discussing the four behaviors that destroy marriage. It concludes with hopeful advice for changing the "script."]

❖ Organizer statements

Rather than a thesis statement as an assertion of thought, writers sometimes announce their organizing plan for what follows. "Organizer" statements often appear near the beginning of a long text, or a new section of a long text. They serve as "promises" of what is to come.

Look for organizer statements, so that you can follow the writer's plan as you read.

Example of organizer statements:

Chapter One
Measurement and Analysis

...(end of p. 2) **In the first parts of this chapter, we look at the work of Tycho Brahe and Johannes Kepler** as an illustration of the value of careful measurement and the subsequent careful analysis of the data

> gathered. In the process, **we introduce some elementary geometry and angular measurement. In the later sections, you learn how to correctly handle numbers and units** so as to maintain proper accuracy when dealing with experimental measurements and the information found in problems…
>
> (Jones & Childers, 1990, *Contemporary College Physics*, Reading, MA: Addison-Wesley)

[Note: The chapter continues for 20+ pages, divided into 8 sections, along the lines promised in the organizer statements.]

❖ Statements of purpose

Instead of a thesis sentence or organizer statements, you might find a writer's statement(s) of purpose near the beginning of a long text. From a writer's aim or purpose, you can figure out the thesis. Statements of purpose also give you a conceptual framework for reading and understanding a text.

Example of statements of purpose:

> Chapter One
> The Problem Is the Process
>
> …(end of p. 3) **This book gives a linguist's view of what makes conversation exhilarating or frustrating.** Through the lens of linguistic analysis of conversational style, **it shows how communication works—and fails to work. The aim is to let you know you are not alone and you're not crazy** [if your talk fails]—**and to give you more choice** in continuing, ending, or improving communication in your private and public life…
>
> (Tannen, 1986, *That's Not What I Meant!* New York: Ballantine)

For a writer's perspective on a thesis, see 002 Making Your Thesis Clear (p. 117).

010 PREVIEWING

❖ What? and Why?

Previewing means to "look ahead," to examine something briefly beforehand. Then you know what to expect.

Before you read a text (an essay, article, story, etc.), you should preview it. This makes you a better reader because (a) you can anticipate what the topic is, (b) you can recall what you already know about it, and (c) you can establish a framework in your mind for a reading.

❖ How to preview

- Notice the larger context of the text. For example, is it a chapter in a sociology textbook? An article in a scientific journal? An excerpt from an article in a magazine published for parents? Given the context, predict the kind of subject matter, the genre of the writing, and the level of difficulty.

- Look at the text itself and ask yourself questions about it. Then predict answers to your questions.

- Look at the pictures and predict what the text is about.

- Recall what you already know about the topic.

- Read the first paragraph and the last paragraph and try to figure out the controlling idea (thesis) of the text.

- Set a purpose for reading. Decide what you hope to find out as you read.

011 QUICKWRITING

❖ When? and How?

After you finish reading something, take up your pen and write quickly about it. Write what you remember, write down the main ideas, make connections to your own experience, say what you think, etc.

❖ Example of quickwriting

> I just read an interview of Sandra Cisneros, written by a newspaper reporter. Cisneros is a Mexican-American poet and writer. Let's see, what do I remember? Oh, yes, her mother taught her to love books, and when she was a child, she started telling stories in her mind. Later, she wrote them down. What's the point of the interview? I think it's that Cisneros wants everyone to know she was lucky to grow up with two languages, two cultures. That's what makes her writing so rich, she says. What does this make me think of? Hmmm, I'm not sure. Oh, yes, Maxine Hong Kingston, who wrote about a very different experience as a child "between" cultures. This gets me thinking about my own childhood. My experience was more like Cisneros's.

❖ Reasons to quickwrite

Quickwriting will do the following:

   a. increase your understanding of what you have read,

   b. help you remember it, and

   c. separate what is clear from what is unclear.

After quickwriting, go back to the original text, look for anything else of importance to you, and, for future reference, add a note or two to your quickwrite.

❖ Questions to ask yourself while quickwriting

  a. What is the text about? (What's the topic?)

  b. What genre is it written in (short story, interview, etc.)?

  c. Who is it written for? What might be the writer's purpose?

  d. What do I remember from my reading?

  e. What is one main point? Are there other points?

  f. What connections can I make to my own experience? To other texts?

g. What question(s) does it answer? What problems or questions does it pose?

h. What does it get me thinking about? Are there any "messages" here?

For quickwriting as a writing strategy, see 005 Quickwriting (p. 123).

012   TAKING NOTES

❖ **Why? and How?**

Taking notes as you read helps you to organize and remember important information. When taking notes, write down only important information, in abbreviated form. Or, if you are doing research and want something specific, write down the information you are looking for.

To keep track of the information, remember to note this:

- author(s)
- date of publication
- title of article
- editor of source, if an edited book
- title of source (book, journal, magazine, etc.)
- volume number or other identification
- page numbers
- place of publication and publisher, if a book.

❖ **Taking notes in a chart**

Here is one type of chart to use:

Main Idea	Important Points
Effects of gender-role stereotyping (p. 50)	• males feel more pressure to achieve • males restrict their emotions • males' stress probably contributes to shorter life expectancy, more heart disease, higher suicide rates, more mental illness • fewer career choices for males and females • females get less help at school

Reference: Landis, J. (1992). *Sociology.* Belmont, CA: Wadsworth. Excerpted in Blanton, L.L., & Lee, L., *Multicultural Workshop: Book 3* (pp. 48-50). Boston: Heinle & Heinle.

---

013   UNDERLINING AS YOU READ

❖ **Why?**

To read well, you need to read actively. This means reading with a pen or pencil in hand. And where is the action? Well, one type of action is to underline what seems most important to your developing sense of the text. Important: If you are reading a text that does not belong to you, do <u>not</u> underline or make any other marks on it. You might take notes instead.

❖ **Underlining to understand a text**

The process of underlining is just as important as *what* you underline. As you underline, your mind is working to separate more important ideas from less important ones. You're awake, alert, and engaged! To underline, you have to get into the flow of ideas and into the writer's mind—especially if you are working on the entire text.

❖ **Example of one reader's underlining**

> Dyslexia is a term used for certain difficulties in learning to read. Dyslexic children are thought to have problems in separating language into distinct sounds at a critical time when this skill is required for learning to read. If a child does not perceive that the spoken language can be split into separate units (sounds, words, sentences), then the child will not perceive the connection between the spoken units and symbols that can be written and read (Webster & McConnell, 1987).

If *you* were underlining the example, would you underline more or less?

❖ **Underlining to "shop" for information**

Another reason to underline is this: you might be shopping for a particular piece of information or a certain idea. Or you might be looking for something useful to you in your own research. Underlining is like a flag to mark the location of useful information.

014   USING CONTEXT TO UNDERSTAND DIFFICULT WORDS

❖ **What?**

When you read, try to figure out the meaning of difficult words by looking at the context—that is, other words in the sentence or nearby sentences. Like a detective, you look for clues among the other words.

❖ **Why?**

For several reasons, you should use the context of your reading to understand difficult words:

a. Using the context will save you time. Stopping every time you don't know a word will cost you hours in homework time. Plus, stopping will interrupt your thinking—your understanding—of whatever you're reading.

b. Chances are it will improve your understanding of the text in front of you. This is because meanings of words change according to context, so a dictionary definition might not even help. Are you skeptical? Take, for example, the simple word "run":

The batter hit a home run.

I had to run to the store for milk.

My sister was upset because she had a run in her brand new stockings.

The manager of my office runs a tight ship.

I'm going to run my computer program this weekend.

I wonder who'll run for president in the next election. And so on.

Now are you convinced?

❖ Common context clues to look for

a. Look for definitions of unusual words to be set off by a comma or commas.

Example:

The way in which caffeine and related compounds work is something of a mystery, but biochemical studies have suggested that these compounds block <u>adenosine, a chemical messenger that occurs naturally in the body.</u>

b. Also look for definitions to follow in separate sentences.

Example:

It was at this time that An Wang invented the <u>magnetic core. This device was a basic part of computer memory</u> until the use of microchips in the late 1960s.

c. Look for actions that illustrate what words mean.

Example:

The old woman's two sons were <u>peddlers.</u> The older one <u>sold umbrellas</u> and the younger <u>sold straw shoes.</u>

d. Look for sentence structures that compare or contrast. If you understand one half, you will have a good idea of the other half.

Example:

My nephew <u>loved the first story, but he despised the second</u> one.

<u>Although she seemed uptight</u> at first, as time passed I realized <u>she was nice.</u>

e. If unfamiliar words appear in a series, but you recognize some of the words, then you will have a general idea of what is going on.

Example:

The class was divided into two groups…One was discussing a <u>collection of materials brought in by a local builder: two-by-fours, plasterboard, nails of different sizes, insulation, vinyl siding, shingles.</u>

f. Notice words that signal cause and effect/result. If you understand part of the "equation," then you will have some idea of the other part.

Example:

Gardner (1994) points out that our <u>culture values some human abilities at the expense of others and that, as a result, we often fail to develop our children's potential.</u>

g. Look for examples. They will help you "get" the meaning of words that name classes or categories.

Example:

Adults who are successful in the roles of <u>dancer, mime, athlete, actor, clown, and comedian</u> are those who <u>possess bodily-kinesthetic intelligence.</u>

h. Notice "gifts" from writers who translate for readers by paraphrasing or offering synonyms of difficult words.

Example:

According to one researcher, the secret of marital bliss resides in a simple notion: <u>positive assortative mating. In other words, marry someone like yourself</u> (Drexler, 1993).

i. Look at visual clues, such as charts, tables, diagrams. Often, complex words and ideas are presented visually, especially in college textbooks.

---

015   WRITING MARGIN NOTES

❖ Why? and What?

Writing notes in the margin of your book helps you to read actively and critically. The process creates a "dialog" between you and the writer, and between you and yourself. **Note:** We are <u>not</u> suggesting you write margin notes in a book that does not belong to you!

As you write notes in the margin, ask yourself questions like these:

What am I thinking ?

What am I recalling from my own experience?

What do other texts say?

What's going on here?

Why am I confused?

What is my reaction?

What would X (Freud, Shakespeare, my mother, etc.) say about this?

❖ Examples of margin notes

a. (Consciously react to the text.)

"Great idea!" "I"m glad that's not me!" "I feel sorry for her!" "Hmmm, I don't think that's such a great idea!"

b. (Write down questions as you read.)

"Why are they doing that?" "What happens next?" "What will the results be?" "What is the main idea here?"

c. (Connect your experience to the text.)

"The same thing happened to me!" "My parents didn't think this way." "No, it was different for me."

d. (Connect ideas from other texts.)

"Just like in Maya Angelou's poem: differences aside, we are all members of the human family."

CRITICAL THINKING STRATEGIES

016   ANALYZING

❖ What?

When you analyze something, you examine it under a microscope, so to speak. You study it from every angle to see (a) what it is, (b) how it works, (c) how everything fits together, and (d) why it is the way it is.

When analyzing, you want to know causes, effects, reasons, purposes, or consequences. In analyzing a piece of writing, you may want to know how the writer put it together, or achieved the effect she or he achieved.

To analyze, ask yourself these questions:

who?	*what?*	*when?*
where?	*why?*	*how?*

❖ Example of analyzing a concept

Excerpt from a newspaper article, analyzing the causes of marital success:

> For the first time, researchers are arriving at a consensus on what it takes for a marriage to survive. Like the ingredients of successful marriages themselves, the findings are often surprising….The basic finding is that anger and disagreement are not harmful to a marriage; it's when that anger is blended with contempt and defensiveness that it's very destructive…
>
> (Bass, 1993, *The Boston Globe*)

❖ Analyzing a text

Teachers may expect you to analyze what you read. To analyze a written text (such as the text excerpted on page 144), ask yourself questions like these:

a. What/who is it about?

> *Example:* successful marriage

b. Who is the intended audience?

> *Example:* general newspaper-reading audience

c. What is the writer's purpose?

> *Example:* perhaps to inform couples whose marriage might be in trouble

d. What is the issue?

> *Example:* What destroys a marriage? Or (the other side of the coin) what does it take for a marriage to survive?

e. How would you characterize the writing (of the complete text)?

> *Example:* The article is difficult, but not too difficult. It is based on scientific research, yet it appeals to a general newspaper audience. How? It relies on concrete examples to explain abstract ideas.

f. What does it all mean? Is there a "message" (in the longer text)?

> *Example:* Married couples need to develop a shared style of communication that honors both partners' need for love and respect.

g. How can I connect it to other texts?

> *Example:* Another article in the Boston Globe (1993), *The Secrets of Marital Bliss,* seems to contradict Bass's article, but actually they both talk about sharing.

h. How can I apply this to what I know?

Example: The couple that lives next door to me fights all the time, but they must fight without "contempt and defensiveness," because they seem to love each other very much.

When you write, your readers need to be able to answer questions like these.

---

017   APPLYING WHAT YOU KNOW

❖ **What?**

"Applying what you know" means taking ideas from one context and using them to understand or explain something in another context. This is what learning is all about. For example, you experience something in daily life, and you then use that experience to explain or understand something you come across in your psychology textbook.

Much of what you know comes from "informal" learning, from life experience. And your experience includes all your travels, jobs, family occasions, books you've read, movies you've seen, etc. Put another way, you have learned much more than you have been "taught." All of this you can apply to your college learning.

❖ **Applying reading to life**

Of course, you can apply what you learn from reading to life, or from life to your reading:

Example:

You read this:

> Medical studies show that sick people get well faster if they feel cared for and loved.

You apply the idea to your own life:

> Remembering your sick uncle, you realize you haven't contacted him lately. Based on what you have read, you decide to visit and telephone him more often. Maybe the added attention will contribute to his recovery.

❖ **Applying ideas "across" texts**

In college writing, you need to apply your learning from one text to another.

Example:

You read an idea from sociologist Judson Landis (1992):

> "Like other roles, gender roles are learned through the socialization process…[In Western culture,] the male is restricted in how he may show emotion: He is strong and silent, he does not show weakness, and he keeps his feelings under careful rein, at least outwardly…"

Then you read an essay on the same topic by Samir Khalaf, a concerned parent (1995):

> "I could see him fret as [Lebanese] relatives and friends he has not seen for two years try, in vain, to solicit a hug or a kiss on the forehead. The reluctant denial has been transformed into a boast, that he is now an 'American' boy."

You apply what you know from one text to another, something like this:

> Khalaf's (1995) experience with his son, George, is a perfect example of what Landis (1992) is talking about. As George becomes socialized into American culture, he becomes increasingly reluctant to show emotions. He must think that he has to keep his feelings under "careful rein," as Landis says, in order to be seen as an "American" boy. It's sad that George is losing the spontaneous expression of his Lebanese culture.

018   CLASSIFYING

❖ What?

"Classifying" means arranging and organizing into groups, classes, segments, or categories. The process of classifying separates, for example, *good* from *not-so-good, cause* from *effect,* or *physical traits* from *personality traits.*

❖ Classifying by sameness of kind

To classify, you need to find a central principle that makes organizing possible. In other words, your classification system must be based on a *sameness of kind.* For example, human beings might be classified (and described) according to (a) physical appearance and (b) personality because both are human traits. It wouldn't work as a serious classification to divide up human beings according to (a) personality and (b) the cars they drive, because these are different kinds of criteria. It might, however, create a basis for a humorous and/or creative essay! (See below.)

❖ Classifying by difference of kind: creating metaphors for writing

When you divide your subject matter according to a principle not normally applied, you create a *metaphor* for writing. A metaphor is a "figure of speech," with qualities being transferred from the object normally possessing those qualities to another object, not normally thought about that way.

In the example on the next page, a writer writes about her friends *as if* they were financial investments and she were the investor. She uses the idea of friends as investments as a metaphor and then classifies her "investments."

Example of a writer using a classifying metaphor:

Friends

In her essay "Friends, Good Friends—And Such Good Friends," Judith Viorst creates a zillion categories for friendships. For her, some friendships are based on convenience, some are based on current shared interests, some on past shared history, some on accidental "crossing-of-paths," and on and on. Such trivial mental activity is beyond me.

I have just two categories of friends, and the only difference between the two is time, and lots of work. The short-term, low-investment category is a large and fluid group made up of people I've met since I moved to New Orleans eighteen months ago. My New Orleans friends are mostly classmates in my writing courses, people who see and critique my writing, and whose writing I see and critique.

These low-investment friendships are delightfully intense and serious at times, but also volatile and potentially disappointing. This is because we often know each other better through reading each other's writing than we do through honest time spent together. Such knowledge and familiarity, without necessarily the investment created through conversation and shared experience, can create stresses that only some friendships can withstand.

The long-term, high investment category is primarily made up of people I left behind when I moved to New Orleans. This is a steady and lean group, whose numbers can be counted on one hand. They are friends who know me, love me, and who can be counted on for anything, even though they live 1500 miles away and I see them only twice a year. I know these friends from the way they wash dishes to the way they choose a restaurant or drink their coffee. Every one of them was once a new person in my life, lingering in the low-investment category, and then slowly revealing him- or herself through conflict as much as companionship. The transition from low-investment to high-investment takes just that—*investment.* And the work is hard.

—*Linda Treash*
Student, University of New Orleans

❖ **Another kind of classifying: segmenting written texts**

In academic writing, particularly in research papers and journal articles, information is often divided into parts. This helps readers understand the flow of ideas and the writer's thinking. It also helps writers organize their thinking, as they prepare to present their research.

In science and social science writing, the following way of organizing and presenting research (in this order) is commonplace:

a. describing the research: what others need to know as background to understand the research

b. explaining the methods used in the research: how the research was conducted

c. presenting the findings: reporting and interpreting what went on (often written in the "narrative" present, especially in the social sciences)

d. analyzing the findings: generalizations, both narrow and broad, that can be drawn from the interpretations

e. concluding the presentation: applying the findings to other research of its kind, and/or explaining what the researcher can do with the new knowledge (often called "applications" and "implications")

The plan above "translates" into (sub)headings used in the actual written presentation of the research: *Introduction/Description, Methodology, Findings, Analysis, Conclusion.*

---

019 COMPARING

❖ **What?**

Comparing is one way to analyze a topic: you look for similarities and explain *what, how, or why. How are X and Y similar? What makes them similar? Why might they be similar at certain times and different at others? What are the implications of the similarity?*

Remember, though, that you cannot compare "apples and oranges." In other words, you can only make comparisons *of kind.* Apples and oranges are different kinds of fruit, so a comparison is useless. You can, however, compare lemons and oranges: they are both citrus fruit.

❖ "Compare" vs. "contrast"

Some use the verb "compare" to mean only "find similarities" and the verb "contrast" to mean "find differences." Others, however, use "compare" to refer to *both* similarities *and* differences. Therefore, on an exam, if your botany professor asks you to "compare the processing of three different teas: green, black, and oolong," she probably wants you to discuss both similarities *and* differences. If you are not sure, ask.

❖ A reader's cues to comparing and/or contrasting

Writers might compare by arranging ideas "side by side," especially if they want to emphasize a difference. As you read, look for the opposition of ideas, as in this example:

> **For years, America was called a "melting pot," a place where the customs of many people melted or blended into one American culture.** }
>
> Today, however, some call the country a "salad bowl," a society made up of different peoples and cultures who are "mixed" together, yet remain separate. }

Notice the special language that writers use when comparing and/or contrasting:

> Researchers <u>agree that</u> the most critical task of a marriage is to create a style of communication that honors both partners' need for love and respect (Bass, 1993).

> Researchers find that men in general are <u>much more</u> uncomfortable with conflict in relationships and thus <u>more likely</u> to withdraw from a potential argument (Bass, 1993).

> According to Avshalom Caspi, a psychologist, the secret to happiness in marriage is to marry someone like yourself, <u>while</u> John Gottman, also a professor of psychology, believes it is the ability to handle differences, <u>not</u> similarity, that helps spouses stay together (Drexler, 1993).

As a reader or writer, it might help to *visualize* similarities and differences in a chart. (See 012 Taking Notes in a Chart, p. 138.)

151

❖ **Writing comparatively**

In a literature course or writing class, you might be asked to agree or disagree with ideas in a written text. The prompt might be to simply "discuss." You can do this by telling what, in your opinion, is "wrong" and/or what is "right." You are, in effect, comparing your ideas to those of the text's author. Look at an example below, both the prompt and a writer's response.

> *Prompt:* In her essay "Friends, Good Friends—And Such Good Friends," Judith Viorst categorizes friendships according to the functions they serve, needs they meet, and their levels of intensity and intimacy. Discuss Viorst's view of friendship and compare it to your own.

A writer's response:

In her essay "Friends, Good Friends—And Such Good Friends," Judith Viorst shows her thinking about friendship to be as opportunistic as it is superficial. Viorst's friends hang in a large and varied wardrobe closet, one that she can pick and choose from on a daily basis. For a shopping trip, she can choose a light weight, wrinkle free, easy-to-wear friend. For a conference with her child's teacher, she can choose a thick, warm one, hand-knit of water-repellent wool, although it seems unlikely that Viorst hand-knit the wool herself.

Viorst's classifications are primarily utilitarian, for her convenience only, and they therefore ignore that friendships, like all human relationships, are not articles of clothing—to be used and discarded, at one's convenience. Rather, friendships, like all relationships, are two-lane roads, scattered with all the complications of human beings and human life. Even when the road looks as if it barrels on straight ahead, friendship is a blind drive, full of ridges and dips that require varying speeds. And life experience offers the only road signs.

—Linda Treash
Student, University of New Orleans

---

020   EVALUATING

❖ **What?**

To evaluate, you make a judgment. *Interesting or boring? A success or a failure? Of major or minor importance? True or false?* You evaluate whenever you answer these questions.

Your evaluation is your opinion. There are no right or wrong answers to matters of evaluation. However, when you evaluate, you need to explain your logic and support your claim. It's not good enough to say something is so just because you say it is. You have to persuade your reader/listener with a well-reasoned and clearly explained argument.

❖ **Example of evaluating to persuade others**

Task:

Decide what's important in a marriage.

State your premise:

Honesty is important in a marriage.

Explain your logic:

• A solid relationship needs to be built on trust.
• To be trustworthy, a spouse has to be honest.
• If a spouse cheats or lies, trust is destroyed, and the relationship suffers.

Illustrate from your experience:

I once knew a young couple. In fact, they were close friends of mine. They promised to trust each other and always tell the truth. One day, the wife discovered that her husband had been cheating on her from the very beginning of their marriage. He had had numerous affairs, while she had remained completely faithful to him. Needless to say, she was devastated. Her trust in her husband was broken, and the couple subsequently divorced.

❖ Evaluating others' ideas, others' writing

You may also need to evaluate others' written ideas. Here are some of the questions you may need to ask yourself:

	YES	NO
• Is the topic clear?	❏	❏
• Do I know what's going on?	❏	❏
• Does the writer give enough information?	❏	❏
• Are the ideas clearly explained and supported?	❏	❏
• Does the writer make the topic interesting?	❏	❏
• Can I follow the writer's thinking?	❏	❏
• Can I sense the presence of the writer?	❏	❏
• Overall, is the piece well-written?	❏	❏

When you evaluate, it always helps to work with others and compare opinions. That way, you get accustomed to explaining what you mean. (See also 006 Revising, p. 124, for questions to use in evaluating others' writing.)

---

021 INTERPRETING

❖ What?

To interpret means to decide on the meaning of something. For example, *I interpret your nod to mean that you agree with me (Newbury House Dictionary of American English,* 1996, p. 455). Here, a nod is interpreted as agreement.

When you interpret something, you also need to consider its *context* and what you think is its intended meaning. So, if you consider context in the example above, maybe a nod does not "mean" agreement. It depends on which part of the world you're in, which culture, right?

General questions to ask yourself:

- What does X mean?
- What does X mean in the context of…(World War II? urban America? a woman's life? Moroccan culture? etc.)

❖ Interpreting artistic work

When you interpret a book, film, or other artistic works, you might first describe the work briefly. Then ask yourself these questions:

- What is the message? Or, what are the messages?
- What is Y (the filmmaker, the artist, the writer) saying?

Example of interpreting an artistic work:

> De Sica's film masterpiece, *The Garden of the Finzi-Continis*, reveals the brutality of anti-Jewish sentiment and government policy in Italy during the Second World War. As in any work of art, the message of this film strikes the viewer as unavoidable truth. Here, De Sica is saying that the hateful heart is just as stubborn as the hopeful heart. The evil of hatred eventually sweeps over the garden wall destroying the family, who deny its existence until too late to save themselves.

❖ Interpreting ideas

When you interpret someone's words, first identify them by quoting or paraphrasing them. (See 004 Paraphrasing, p. 121, and 008 Using Quotations, p. 129.) Then say what the words mean to you. To support your interpretation, present facts and details from the work itself, and/or from your own experience.

Example of interpreting someone's idea:

> The writer Sandra Cisneros says that "people's cultures are what make them special" (1991). To me, this means that people's language and customs give them a unique identity. A perfect example is Cisneros herself. Her special stories emerge from the richness of her own Mexican-American heritage.

022   SYNTHESIZING

❖ What?

Synthesizing is the process of pulling information and ideas together from different sources. This is particularly important in college writing.

When pulling together ideas/information, you create something new, framed by your own thinking. In fact, unless others' information/ideas are the *topic* of your writing, you put your ideas in the foreground and let others' ideas support yours.

❖ Illustration of the process of synthesizing

Scenario:

Interested in researching the topic of marriage, you set about collecting information. You read about the work of Avshalom Caspi, a psychologist at the University of Wisconsin (Drexler, *The Boston Globe,* 1993). You also read about the research of John Gottman, of the University of Washington (Bass, *The Boston Globe,* 1993).

You have your own observations to draw from; plus, you seek out the ideas of your classmates. After taking notes, thinking, brain-storming, and doing some quickwriting, you create a synthesis, such as the one below.

Synthesis:

According to Avshalom Caspi (1993), the secret to happiness in marriage is to marry someone like yourself. John Gottman, also a psychologist, believes it is the ability to handle differences, not similarity, that keeps spouses together (1993). To me, these claims are compatible. To handle their differences, a couple has to create a shared style of communication. This means they are "alike" in at least one aspect of their marriage, perhaps the most important one. I once knew a couple who…

Grammar Workshops

Grammar Workshop 1a

a. The purpose of an adjective clause is to give more information about a person or thing. This information often helps you to identify which person or thing you are talking about.

b. You can begin an adjective clause with the words "who," "that," or "which."

c. You can use "who" when you are talking about people. You use "that" when you are talking about people or things. You can also use "which" when you are talking about things.

d. You can leave out the words "who" and "that" when they are not the subject of the adjective clause.

e. The first example has a singular verb because it is describing "a man," which is singular. The second example has a plural verb because it is describing "people," which is plural.

Grammar Workshop 1b

a. An appositive gives more information about a person or thing.

b. In the third sentence, the information in the appositive is necessary. You need this information to understand who the writer is talking about. In the other two sentences, the information in the appositive is not necessary. You know who or what the writer is talking about without this information. Writers don't use commas when the appositive provides necessary information.

Grammar Workshop 2a

a. 1) noun clause: there are; main clause: Judith Viorst / suggests
   2) noun clause: he / had decided; main clause: the President / said
   3) noun clause: essay / is; main clause: I / think
   4) noun clause: essay / is; main clause: I / think
   5) noun clause: world / was; main clause: people / used to
   6) noun clause: world / was; main clause: people / used to

b. It tells what Viorst suggests.

c. Yes, it is. When the word "that" introduces a noun clause, it is often omitted.

Grammar Workshop 2b

a. In academic writing, we often use the present tense to report what someone said or wrote—especially when talking about general truths.

b. In the first three examples, the writer is reporting on something expressed in a specific piece of writing. In examples 4 and 5, the writer is reporting what someone said in the past.

Grammar Workshop 3b

a. Example 1: Dividing / assigns
   Example 2: Focusing / is
   Example 3: Growing up / can be

b. Using a gerund at the beginning of a sentence sometimes helps the writer to make connections between sentences. This helps the reader to follow the writer's ideas. Also, in English, the information at the beginning of a sentence gets emphasis. Using a gerund might be the best way to put the emphasis on the right information. Writers might also begin a sentence with a gerund in order to provide sentence variety in their writing.

Grammar Workshop 4a

a. You use a comma when the adverb clause comes before the main clause. You don't use a comma when the adverb clause comes after the main clause.

b. You can begin an adverb clause with words such as *when, since, although, because.*

c. The location of the adverb clause depends in part upon the information in the preceding sentence.

Grammar Workshop 4b

a. were inspired / inspired; had finished / Having finished; value / Valuing

b. In the last sentence, the subject of the adverb clause and the subject of the main clause are different.

Grammar Workshop 5a

a. In the first group, "stimulant" is a noun and "stimulates" is a verb. In the second group, "consumption" is a noun; "consume" is a verb; "consuming" is a gerund; "to consume" is an infinitive.

b. Knowing the different forms of a word provides you with alternative ways to express an idea in writing. When you are able to express the same information in different ways, you can make choices that will help your reader follow your ideas. Knowing the different forms of words also makes it easier to paraphrase someone else's words and ideas.

Grammar Workshop 5b

a. Caffeine; The alkaloid caffeine; one…stimulant; one stimulant; One thing

b. 2, 2, 1, 1, 1

Grammar Workshop 5c

a. The first part of each sentence helps the reader follow the writer's ideas from one sentence to the next.

b. The beginning of a sentence usually tells the reader what the sentence is about. It may also make a connection back to something mentioned earlier.

Grammar Workshop 6a

a. Parallel forms are words or phrases in a sentence that have the same grammatical function. For example, in the first sentence, both the words "monopolized" and "prevented" function as main verbs in the sentence. Because they have the same function, they also have the same form (the simple past tense).

b. It helps your reader follow your ideas.

Grammar Workshop 6b

a. These words and phrases help connect one sentence to the next.

b. Some other examples of conjunctive adverbs are: *above all, in other words, for instance, also, first, in contrast,* etc.

Grammar Workshop 7

a. The first paragraph has more sentence variety.

b. The first paragraph seems easier to follow because one sentence seems connected to the next.

CREDITS

PHOTOS/ILLUSTRATIONS

pp. 1, 96   Michael Williams

p. 2   Photofest

p. 73   Bob Daemmrich/The Image Works

pp. 13, 77, 87 Mike Burggren

TEXT

p. 7   "Night" by Bret Lott, from *A Dream of Old Leaves* by Bret Lott, 1989, Viking Penguin, a division of Penguin Books USA, Inc. Reprinted with permission.

pp. 15-18   "Friends, Good Friends-and Such Good Friends," by Judith Viorst, 1977. Originally appeared in *Redbook*. Reprinted by permission of Lescher & Lescher, Ltd.

pp. 40-44   "7 Keys to Learning" by Phyllis La Farge. Appeared in *Parents* magazine, February 1994. Reprinted with permission

pp. 55-65   "Stimulating Beverages" from *Economic Botany: Plants in Our World*, second edition, by Beryl Brintnall Simpson and Molly Conner Ogorzaly, McGraw-Hill, Inc., NY. Reprinted with permission.